FLIP
FOR DECORATING

Elizabeth Mayhew

FLIP!
FOR DECORATING

A PAGE-BY-PAGE, PIECE-BY-PIECE, ROOM-BY-ROOM GUIDE TO TRANSFORMING YOUR HOME

BALLANTINE BOOKS NEW YORK

TO TIM, MADELEINE, AND CHARLIE — WITHOUT YOU, OUR HOUSE WOULD NOT BE A HOME

contents

WHEN
FRIENDS
CALL ME
FOR
DECORATING
ADVICE,
I KNOW
THEY'RE
LOOKING
FOR
NO-FUSS
SOLUTIONS.

introduction

There are infinite possibilities in home décor. The vast spectrum of choices can be exciting, but more often than not, the options are overwhelming. And believe me, whether you're ready for a major house overhaul, or simply need to enliven a tired living room, the biggest gaff you can make in decorating is putting it off. *Flip! for Decorating* will help you make simple and achievable decisions about decorating, whether you're starting with an empty house or are ready to liven up your already furnished apartment.

When friends call me for decorating advice, I know they're looking for no-fuss solutions: the perfect gray paint, a sofa she'll love forever, or a quick way to hang art before a party. I never reply with a laundry list of design rules, instead I'll send her a one-line e-mail, "Benjamin Moore, Owl Gray in flat finish." That gets her on her way to the hardware store and toward overall design improvements.

You're probably the same way—you don't have time to comb through 300 swatches of gray paint or to mock up a few curtain styles before making a decision. So now I've done the heavy lifting for you. As a longtime decorating editor, it's my job to know everything on the market—and to distill that into a short list of fail-safe choices that will get your home looking pretty, polished, and unequivocally *you* in a snap.

Flip! for Decorating kicks off by laying the groundwork for your home's decorating scheme. Chapter 1 spells out the fundamentals of color, specifically, how to choose the perfect paint for a single room or a harmonious palette for your entire home. Paint is the fastest, easiest, and most dramatic way to transform a room. So to make it even easier, I've included a list of my favorite, no-fail paint colors to help you narrow down your choices.

Chapter 2 focuses on window treatments, teaching you how to select curtains or shades that bring new life to any window. Both chapters are packed with simple, effective ways to update your interiors. Tips like painting the ceiling a lighter color than the walls and hanging custom-made or store bought curtains high above the window frame will make any room seem more spacious. Before investing in a new sofa or rug, consider the techniques in Color and Windows—you'll be surprised how changing the wall color or dressing up a window treatment can make a room look brand-new.

Chapters 3 through 6 focus on the four most decorated rooms in your home: the living room, dining room, family room, and bedroom. Each chapter begins with a section about the biggest, most important (and usually costliest) piece of furniture for that particular room. Think sofa, dining table, and bed. Second only to wall paint and windows, these marquee pieces of furniture make the biggest impact on a room. Even if you're not in the market for a new sofa, skim through the section to learn where to place the one you already have to help reinvent your room.

Additional pieces of furniture and accessories are explained throughout the chapters. Each time an item is added to the room, a section called *Basics* will give you information about how it's used in the room and tips for buying it. *Typecasting* breaks down the merits of specific types of furniture and clarifies questions of style, such as when you should use a round dining table verses a square one.

And you can even let your fingers do the walking. Unlike other decorating books, *Flip! for Decorating* shows you the progression of decorating a room step-by-step. Just use your thumb to flip through chapters 3 through 6 and you'll watch four rooms assembled one piece of furniture at a time!

As you "flip" through the book, look for recurring sidebars, such as *Measure for Measure*, which illustrates the proper dimensions and measurements for furniture, rugs, and lighting, and *Educated Consumer* and *Test Drive* for quick shopping tips. *Panic Button, If there's One Thing You Do, and Why Not Try,* will give you solutions if you are stumped, stymied, or need to add a quick jolt of style to a room, and fast. Each of these chapters end with *Finishing Touches* aimed at teaching you styling tricks so that all areas of your home, from bookcase to bed, look natural but pulled together—and even magazine-ready.

Luckily for you, it's a great time to shop for your home. Today you can buy everything from fabric by the yard to custom upholstery, to chandeliers to hand-woven rugs with just a click or a call. New styles of furniture and accessories appear (and disappear) as fast as seasonal fashions: When patent leather hits the runway in Milan, it's only a matter of weeks before it shimmies its way into showrooms around the world. It's easy to fall for trends (I do it, too), but try to use them sparingly, like you do in your wardrobe. Resist the urge to buy a sofa decked out in the trend *du jour* and, instead, indulge in inexpensive art or accessories like colored vases and blankets that satisfy your urge but won't feel "last season" before the check clears.

Decorating your home is, in a lot of ways, like getting dressed, with similar factors to take into account. When you buy clothing, I'm sure you consider what colors look good on you, what styles fit your body type, and when and where you plan to wear the item.

It's the same when choosing a decorating scheme for your home. Think about your personal space. Consider the size and architectural style of your home, and the climate of your surroundings. What fits your lifestyle? Do you frequently host parties or do you work from home? What makes sense for your stage in life? Are you a homeowner with children or fresh out of school on an assistant's budget?

The more realistic you are about how you live, the better the choices you'll make for your home. Most of us falter when we pick objects that are too aspirational, such as buying a pair of silk velvet-covered chairs for a home with a new baby or kitten. However, there's no need to forgo flourishes of fancy just because you have pets or children; just scale it back and luxuriate with silk-velvet throw pillows instead. If you can't afford the eight matching dining room chairs that you love, why not buy two and place them at the heads of your table? Mixing and matching furniture of different styles is a great way to make a room look modern and fresh.

So what are you waiting for? Don't hesitate to buy that perfect chair or alter those window treatments. You're only a few pages away from decorating bliss.

Now get ready to FLIP!

FLIP!

FOR DECORATING

color

in this chapter you will learn:
no-fail wall and trim colors
how to make a room appear larger
when to use wallpaper instead of paint
when to paint your home yourself and when to hire a pro
the best paint colors available

**THERE IS
NO SUCH
THING AS A
BAD
COLOR,
ONLY BAD
COLOR
COMBINATIONS.**

Painting your walls is, without a doubt, the single most transformative tool in all of interior design — and one of the most flexible. Its impact is immediate, changing the mood of a room and your perception of its size. Use it to spotlight overlooked details in a home's architecture or to make ho-hum furnishings spring to life. The worst faux pas you can make is to just accept the standard default white paint that was slapped on the walls by your contractor or landlord. Nothing makes a room feel more unfinished. Your new home awaits you; it's only a trip to the hardware store away.

While painting a room is easy, choosing a color can be a challenge. But take note: There is no such thing as a bad color, only bad color combinations. Take mauve and teal. Who would ever conceive of pairing them? A former editor of mine called the duo the "colors of a bruise." It's not a flattering combination, but it is avoidable.

Unfortunately for most people, decorating is not as easy as dressing. If a shirt clashes with a pair of pants, you just change one of them, but once you have committed a wall or sofa to a certain destiny, it takes more time than a wardrobe change to remedy it. Which is why we find ourselves laboring over tiny fabric swatches and paint samples, wondering if one color goes with another.

To simplify your options, try this foolproof recipe: Pair color with white. Choose absolutely any hue on the color wheel—for paint or fabric—and pair it, trim it, or surround it with white and the result will be a fresh and sophisticated look that's a dynamic backdrop for any design scheme.

the power of paint

Painting is the easiest, least expensive way to beautify your rooms. That said, it can also be an overwhelming process as the options are limitless. And what looks good on a one-inch paint chip can look very different when you've dipped a whole room in it.

What goes wrong between loving the paint swatch and hating the painted room? It usually comes down to light. The way a room receives (or doesn't receive) light is the biggest factor in how you perceive color. Too much light and paint loses its saturation and looks like a photo that's been overexposed by a flashbulb. Not enough and color falls flat on its face, lifeless. While window coverings can help diffuse this conundrum, you can also prepare for it by taking a practice run.

The simplest way to judge a given color is to try it out. Most companies sell small, inexpensive sample pots for exactly this purpose. Pick your favorite color (or colors) and paint your walls with a few 12-inch square patches. Alternatively, you can paint the color on a few painters' canvases or pieces of foamcore board (you can purchase both at an arts and crafts store) and place them around the room in question. Painting several areas versus just one will give you the truest representation, because while paint reacts one way to direct sunlight, it can look completely different in softer, diffused light. Live with the patches for a few days and watch how they change from morning to night. Quality paint will take on different hues at different times of day.

working with (or without) light

There are likely some rooms in your home that are blasted with daylight and others that rely solely on artificial light. Common knowledge would have it that dark rooms should be painted in light colors to counteract their natural dimness. But consider the opposite. Pale colors tend to feel dingy and flat in low light, so why not use the shadowy corners to your advantage and try a rich hue like dark brown or something regal like aubergine. Rooms that are used solely in the evening, such as a dining room, respond especially well to this treatment (see page 15): Saturated colors bring complexity and warmth to a space. You won't believe that you once thought low light was a detriment.

(see page 15)

LIGHTBULB

IF YOU'RE STUMPED ABOUT HOW TO MIX COLORS WITHIN A ROOM OR FOR NEIGHBORING ROOMS, SIMPLY CHOOSE COLORS FROM ONE PAINT SWATCH, WHICH OFFERS ANYWHERE FROM THREE TO SEVEN HUES PER CARD. FOR EXAMPLE, IF YOU'RE SMITTEN WITH THE BENJAMIN MOORE HISTORICAL COLOR WYTHE BLUE (HC-143), THEN LOOK ABOVE AND BELOW ON THE PAINT STRIP, STRATTON BLUE (HC-142) AND PALLADIAN BLUE (HC-144)— THEY'RE GUARANTEEDTO BE COMPLEMENTARY.

go with the flow

Think twice before painting just one room cardinal red while the rest of the house is coated in vanilla. Either the whole house will look unfinished (which is okay if that's true) or it will appear as if that room was your one "experiment," which seems a bit insincere. Either way, it'll feel jarring and out of place.

Keep in mind how the color of one room flows into another room. For rooms that open onto one another or in open rooms with no obvious divisions, plan on keeping the room color the same or opt for the same color a shade lighter or a shade darker; this will keep the rooms from looking disjointed.

For rooms with more finite boundaries, look to colors that share a commonality. It's as easy as consulting a color wheel. Sea green to green to yellow works. So does pale blue to cream to pink. Maintaining the same color trim—white—will also help unify rooms. So will colored objects, furniture, and art; using bursts of color from one room in an adjacent room will unite the two spaces.

breaking the rules

You've probably inherited some notions about paint colors already and about that miracle-worker white paint especially. Maybe you've heard it's the only appropriate color for small spaces and for ceilings. Or that rich or dark colors make a room feel smaller. Throw those concepts out the window; life is too short to play it safe with white paint.

Normally, our perception of a room's size comes from seeing where ceiling meets the walls and walls meet each other. It's easy to pick out the boundaries of a room when it's painted white and loaded with dark corners. Now, consider coating the walls (and maybe the ceiling) in a saturated color. All of a sudden those telling lines have disappeared before our eyes. Shadows become nuances—and when you're thinking about nuances, you're not obsessing about size.

Painting four walls and ceiling one color is best for bedrooms (so you can actually enjoy staring at the ceiling), bathrooms, and any room that's blessed with high ceilings.

tricked out

With a few gallons of paint, you can be your own sorcerer. Here are a few ways to transform your rooms with a brush and a roller.

Declutter a room: Paint walls the same hue as your sofa or largest piece of furniture and watch the furniture recede into space.

Spotlight art or photographs: Paint a dark or bright color on a wall featuring framed pictures, objects, or books. They'll pop from the contrast (see page 138).

Raise the ceiling: Coat the ceiling in a tone or two lighter than the walls—but not necessarily white. It will appear higher.

Highlight shapely furniture: A chair with a spectacular openwork back or a curvy sofa can be amplified by painting the wall a contrast color (see page 15). Lavender, powder pink, and robin's egg blue help dark wood look its best, while more saturated colors will let a crisp white sofa shine.

Sleep tight: The bedroom is the only room where you fully see the ceiling. Dipping your whole bedroom in one hue, such as pale celadon, guarantees a cozy, enveloping sensation each night. If you're stuck on white ceilings, pick a hue that borders on powder blue for the illusion of a cloudless sky.

edit your choices

The color choices most paint companies offer is, in a word, overwhelming. And the average person will only have an opportunity to test a handful of colors in a lifetime, but for decorating and style editors like me, it's a regular hobby. I've tried so many colors—for photo shoots, in friends' houses, and in my own home—that I've whittled down the bunch to a hot list of no-fail favorites.

I tend to use paint from two companies: Benjamin Moore and Farrow & Ball. Benjamin Moore paint is easy to find and it offers a huge array of colors, all of which are reasonably priced, easy to apply, and quite durable. Farrow & Ball, a small British firm that has a growing presence online and in the United States, offers a tightly edited color palette of less than 150 colors. The paints are made traditionally, with a much higher concentration of pigment, giving them noticeably greater depth and complexity. And they have a price tag to reflect that ($75 per gallon vs. Benjamin Moore's $35). I like Farrow & Ball's entire palette; each hue is spot on. But when you're wading through the staggering inventory of a Benjamin Moore, you'll need a bit of direction.

Here are my favorites.

ABOVE ALL, CHOOSE COLORS YOU LIKE. DON'T FALL PREY TO THE COLORS OF THE SEASON (THEY'LL CHANGE BEFORE YOU'VE PRIED OFF THE LID OF THE PAINT CAN) AND DON'T SUBJECT YOURSELF TO "SAFE" COLORS (OR ECCENTRIC ONES) THAT DON'T SUIT YOU. HEED THE WISDOM OF YOUR CLOSET: IF YOUR FRIENDS KNOW YOU AS THE WOMAN WHO WEARS HEAD-TO-TOE CORAL, THEN THAT SHADE MIGHT ALSO BE YOUR DINING ROOM'S DESTINY.

red:
benjamin moore
million dollar red
#2003-10

Reds are difficult because they are often mixed with too much blue or too much yellow. This red strikes a fine balance. I particularly like it in dining rooms because it gives a warm, flattering cast to skin tones. Don't you want your guests to look their best at the dining table? It can also bring a note of coziness to a family room or library.

green:
benjamin moore
potpourri green
#2029-50

Green, particularly a pale green like this one, looks great
in kitchens where food and colors abound. Green goes with
everything—why do you think chefs use herbs as garnish?
This paint color serves the same purpose; it's fresh, crisp,
and not too saturated. It can also stand in as a neutral
color. Some colors in the green family can be tricky to live
with (paging Granny Smith), but earthy and pale tones are
calming and fresh, making them winners in bathrooms, too.

brown:
benjamin moore
wood grain brown
#2109-30

My favorite color in the world is chocolate brown. I like it paired with pink, blue, red, yellow, green, lavender, and even black. It is hard to find a good brown—they often have too much red in them, which causes them to look like the color of a melted Hershey's Kiss (trust me, it's not an appealing wall color). I prefer browns that have a gray undertone, which gives them a touch of refinement. This one's found in my dining room.

yellow:
benjamin moore
hawthorne yellow
#HC-4

This yellow works well in rooms and hallways that are exposed to little natural light because it brings an element of sun. Hawthorne Yellow is neither too lemony (which would mean too green feeling), nor too golden (brown). It's from Benjamin Moore's Historic Charleston collection and is mixed to resemble a paint color found in one of the South Carolina city's most famous historic homes. Yellow can be energizing and motivating, too, but this chip walks the line between tranquil and turbocharged.

gray:
benjamin moore
gray owl,
#2137-60

After using it in my bedroom, I've recommended this color to several friends and many of them like it so much that they've used it throughout their houses. This hue is less predictable than a blue would be, yet just as soothing. It's extremely adaptable to all color schemes; just like a favorite gray skirt or pair of pants, it goes with everything. It's also versatile because it's so pale; in fact, many people are bound to read this color as "white."

blue:
benjamin moore
bird's egg
#2051-60

This blue has a clean gray tint, which makes it more
sophisticated than other "baby" blues. Blues, like greens, are
a natural backdrop for all colors and styles of decorating
because blue and green are the most prevalent colors found
in nature—think sky and grass—and go with everything
from brown and black to red and orange. I consider blue to
be interchangeable with white.

greige:
benjamin moore
early morning
mist #1528

Somewhere between gray and beige is this most neutral color. Many years ago when I was working at *House Beautiful* I helped produce a story called "What's Pretty Now," which focused on how "pretty" motifs like flowers and lace were getting fresh modern makeovers. We used this color as a backdrop and it gave an updated, sophisticated look to what could have been a saccharine group of objects and furniture. It is a beautiful backdrop for nearly any decorating scheme.

white
for moldings:
benjamin moore
decorator's white

All the trim and moldings in my apartment are slicked with the semigloss finish of this foolproof white. It's the best white for the job, bar none.

finishing facts

Paint finishes range from chalky to new-car shiny, and, they set the tone for the room. The finish should depend on the function of the room and the condition of your walls. High-traffic rooms benefit from finishes that are eggshell or glossier, while homes and rooms that aren't prone to fingerprints can get away with a flat (or matte) finish. Imperfections are less noticeable in a flat finish. When in doubt, follow the crowd and choose eggshell, the most flexible and most popular finish.

Flat, also called matte, has an elegant, chalky appearance. It works especially well in masking the imperfections on walls and ceilings, which are exposed when a glint of light catches them. It is fairly easy to touch up, but not to clean, so avoid using it in high-traffic areas such as hallways, kitchens, bathrooms, and playrooms.

Eggshell is the most popular and most versatile finish and has just the slightest bit of sheen to make it an easy surface to both wash and touch up.

Satin with its silky finish works well in high-use areas like family rooms, children's rooms, kitchens, and bathrooms. It is easy to clean, but difficult to touch up because any difference in sheen will be apparent.

Semigloss is ideal for trim and moldings because it contrasts handsomely with flat walls. It adds a lift to the room in the same way that frosted eye shadow makes eyes perk up. This finish is durable and easy to clean, which is very important for baseboards and door and window moldings that get bumped and scuffed. It's a good choice for the walls of kitchens and baths. Like a satin finish, semigloss is hard to touch up.

High Gloss provides a glassy finish that is rarely used on walls because it vividly shows imperfections. On trim, moldings, and cabinetry it gives a racy, almost lacquerlike sheen. It is the most durable and easiest to clean of the finishes.

lids off: paints exposed

All interior paints are oil-based or latex. Oil-based paints were the original interior house paints but today most jobs call for latex, which is quick-drying, easy to clean up, and low in VOC's (Volatile Organic Compounds), which are harmful to humans and the environment. While latex is right for walls and ceilings, small details like trim work or wood furniture, for example, still benefit from a coat of oil-based paint. It goes on smoothly, won't leave brush strokes, doesn't usually require more than one coat, and dries into a stronger enamel than latex. Also, if your trim has already been painted with oil (a professional can tell you), you'll need to stick with it, as latex won't adhere. Additionally, a number of environmentally sensitive paints have come on the market in recent years. Low- or no-VOC paint won't emit the harmful gases associated with many paints, and are especially popular for the rooms of babies and children. Farrow & Ball is naturally low in VOC's, as is Benjamin Moore's Eco Spec paint and all products by AFM Safecoat.

EDUCATED CONSUMER

IF YOU'VE FOUND YOUR COLOR INSPIRATION IN REAL LIFE, SAY, FROM A FAVORITE SHIRT OR FLOWER OR FRUIT, BRING IT TO THE HARDWARE STORE OR PAINT SHOWROOM TO HAVE IT MATCHED. A DESCRIPTION OR EVEN A PHOTO IS NOT ENOUGH. SAME GOES FOR FINDING YOUR DREAM HUE IN A MAGAZINE OR BOOK—EVEN IF THE PAINT COLOR IS CREDITED WITH A NAME AND NUMBER. PRINTED IMAGES GO THROUGH LAYERS UPON LAYERS OF RETOUCHING AND THEN PRINTING, WHICH DRAMATICALLY ALTER ITS APPEARANCE. THE MOST RELIABLE WAY TO GET A PERFECT MATCH IS TO SHOW UP WITH YOUR SOURCE IN HAND.

going pro

Don't be intimidated—painting isn't hard. It requires prep work and some patience, but it's fun and rewarding to watch your living room transform in a matter of hours. That said, there are times that it's worth seeking professional help. Kitchen cabinetry, which is studded with hinges and screws, will benefit from a pro's brush, as will ornate trims and moldings in historic homes. For everything else, just roll up your sleeves.

paper pursuits

Wallpaper has enjoyed a renaissance in the past few years and the market is now flooded with offerings that range from dynamic to demure, from the '60s-style metallic geometrics you probably saw in your great aunt's bungalow to quaint and cottagey prints so prevalent in B&Bs. Wallpaper imparts a charming feeling that's hard to replicate with paint. In small rooms, wallpaper can be enchanting, adding a lot of personality. And while it's a great bandage for walls in so-so condition, it can be a challenge to work into a decorating scheme because committing your walls to a paper severely limits your ability to use pattern elsewhere in the room. For every choice you make about color palette, fabrics, and accessories, you must first consider the walls.

There are exceptions, of course. Wallpaper motifs that offer a lot of white space keep the room looking airy and not too overdone. A textured solid paper, such as a straw-colored grass cloth, adds depth to a room without limiting other design possibilities (see page 190). Use your wildest wallpaper whim in bathrooms and powder rooms. You'll love it while you're in the room, but you won't have to spend hours face-to-face with such brazen style.

Installing wallpaper requires help. Don't let anyone convince you that you can hang a complicated pattern—it's too expensive a material to risk botching the job. So consider saving wallpaper for an occasional indulgence. To make a wrong step with paint means just rolling up your sleeves and going at it again, but if it's with paper, it's a pricey predicament.

windows

in this chapter you will learn:

how to choose the right treatment for your windows
how to measure for curtains and shades
how to make small windows appear larger
how to choose the right hardware
how to work with sewing professionals
how to embellish store-bought shades and curtains

WINDOW
TREATMENTS
SHOULD BE
INTERESTING
BUT THEY
SHOULD
NEVER STEAL
THE SHOW.

When I think of window treatments I always think of one of my favorite childhood books, *Amelia Bedelia*, in which author Peggy Parish's kooky housekeeper character interprets—perhaps too literally—her employer's directives to "draw the drapes." So rather than pull the curtains closed as she was asked, Amelia takes out a pen and paper and literally draws a picture of the fancy living room curtains. The scene always struck me as funny not just because of the farcical play on words, but also for the absurd formality of it all: Who really ever draws the draperies? I don't blame Amelia for getting this one wrong. I guess I have always been more of a "let the shade down" kind of girl. I don't like fancy curtains like those of Mrs. Rogers, Amelia's employer. Swags, tassels, fringe, and billowing fabric have always seemed overdone to me, like a prom dress gone awry. (For more about the difference between draperies and curtains, see page 36.) For my own house, I have only ever used Roman shades or simple, floor-length curtain panels; **I keep window treatments tailored, crisp, and elegant and only sometimes add a touch of trim, appliqué, or contrast border.** So just keep curtains simple, but make sure that they fit the window properly: When closed they should fully cover a window while maintaining a few soft folds for volume. It is far worse to hang something too small than to hang nothing at all.

Windows connect us to the outdoors and are a natural gathering spot; they bring sunlight, views, and ventilation to our homes. And design-wise they're vital because they're the most architecturally significant feature of any room.

It's easy to understand the old maxim that windows are the "eyes of the house." Not only do they peer onto the outside world, but, with a little dressing up, they can be a room's most expressive characteristic. Some are tall and graceful, stretching from floor to ceiling, others so small they're practically winking. Some historic houses have 16-pane windows, other modern homes have pane-less windows that span walls. There's a different mood and feeling for each one, but one thing is constant: Save for a demolition, your windows are here to stay.

Luckily, the fabric you pick for your window treatments and the way you mount them offer limitless ways to transform even problem windows into gracious, light-giving sources of beauty.

identifying your needs

REALITY CHECK

BEFORE YOU GET CARRIED
AWAY WITH INTRICATE
PLEATS AND FANCY
EMBELLISHMENTS, JUST
REMEMBER THAT WINDOWS
EXIST TO LET IN
AIR AND LIGHT, AND
WINDOW COVERINGS ARE
THERE TO CONTROL
THOSE ELEMENTS.
THAT'LL HELP KEEP
YOUR WINDOW
DECORATION—AND YOUR
BUDGET—IN CHECK.

First things first. When it comes to window treatments, you need much less than you think. Yes, a room feels unfinished when its panes of glass are barren, but, on the other end of the spectrum, a fussy window is like an elaborate hat on an otherwise smart ensemble: overkill. The idea of dressing a window has been somewhat overstated and oversold. Traditionally, curtains accounted for a huge chunk of the decorating budget (hence the overselling). And while there's a bit of math involved in measuring and making curtains, even the most overwrought curtains are still hewn from fabric.

Blinds, shades, and curtains are the three most popular (and simplest) ways to dress a window, and you're bound to use at least two of those styles in your home, in tandem or solo. Blinds are for light control and are rarely decorative (chunky wood blinds with fabric tape are an exception), while shades offer light control and aesthetics. Lined curtains are vital for blocking light and add a finishing touch to any decorating scheme.

But window coverings are not one size fits all; each room in your house needs a specific prescription. Especially crucial are the needs of the bedroom, where morning sunlight can be more jarring than the piercing cry of an alarm clock. And if you use your living room primarily at night, you'll probably desire a window covering that shields the night glass, which becomes reflective, cold, and dark (and that veils your evening hobbies from nosy neighbors).

If you have historic or architecturally stunning windows in rooms that don't need privacy or light control, skip window coverings altogether. Windows in passages such as a landing or hallway and high windows in a bathroom or kitchen are all good candidates for leaving bare.

While windows pointing east or north are subject to only moderate light, south- and west-facing views are blessed (and challenged) with direct sunlight. And as the seasons change, so will your curtain needs. You might desire less coverage in the winter when sunlight hours dwindle and more protection in summer if you're faced with blisteringly hot rays. The landscape will affect your choice, too. If verdant summer months bring a canopy of leaves over your roof then you've already got an all-natural sunblock.

Walk through each room and envision how you use it. Of each window, ask yourself two questions:

1. What degree of light does this window receive and how much of it do I want to preserve?

2. Is this a view I want to emphasize or one that I'd like to hide?

The answer to those determines the kind of coverage you'll need, from pinpointing the variety (shade, blind, curtain) to possible fabrics and finally the style in which it'll be mounted.

If the view out of the window is worth emphasizing, pick an understated treatment that maximizes the amount of exposed glass and acts as a frame—not the focal point. If you're trying to divert attention from the window, a treatment with more than one layer will help veil the view.

The textiles you choose for your curtains should somehow relate to the colors and textures in the room itself. The feeling and style of window coverings should be in keeping with the mood of the room.

The simplest way to find the right color for window coverings, is to take cues from the paint, carpet, or upholstery. Drawing out a hue from the room's prints, such as on a rug or pillow, is another way to keep it congruous. You can also choose a color that complements or matches a piece of painted furniture, a prominent piece of art, or the braided trim on a chair.

Don't overlook the chance to layer in an interesting texture. If the furnishings are covered in matte-looking linen, consider raw silk or taffeta to brighten the room with a bit of sheen.

shades and blinds

Shades and blinds are two kinds of structured window coverings that can be made from wood, metal, vinyl, or fabric and typically raise and lower with a string-pull, or with a high-tech automated mechanism. Shades and blinds are the most efficient tools for blocking light and can be used alongside curtains or on their own. Though the terms *shades* and *blinds* are often used interchangeably, the two are best distinguished by the fact that blinds are primarily functional, while shades can be both functional and decorative.

typecasting: shades and blinds

For Function

Venetian blinds and honeycomb shades are function-based solutions. Traditionally, these partner with fabric shades or curtains. Alone, they can make a room feel a bit unfinished, but some modern homeowners choose to use them solo because they don't distract from the architecture of a beautiful window frame.

Venetian blinds. These are the most typical version of blinds. Their stacked, horizontal slats are made of vinyl, metal, or wood, and can tilt to fine-tune light control. Venetian blinds are ideal for privacy as the angle of the slats allows light to enter without revealing what's inside. And because you can wash or wipe them, slat blinds are ideal for bathrooms and or kitchens.

Pleated, cellular, and honeycomb shades. These are made from two layers of thin, accordion-fold material that are fused with insulating cells in between (the cross section of one looks like a honeycomb). This energy-efficient solution traps hot or cool air, helping to maintain an ideal climate indoors. This style is offered in many colors, and, if used solo, is apt for modern interiors.

Roller shades. These are simple panels of vinyl or fabric that are either spring-rigged or outfitted with string pulls that roll them up and down. The vinyl variety is ubiquitous and unsightly, but canvas roller shades can look just right in very modern spaces. Look for a medium-weight canvas or any fabric that's stiff but lightweight, which makes for easy rolling.

For Fashion

Generally, shades are a decorative addition to a room, though many thoughtfully constructed models will block light just as effectively as blinds.

Wood blinds. Though technically blinds, these thick, flat slats of wood are appropriate on their own, recalling the tropical simplicity of plantation-style shutters.

Roman shade. This flat fabric panel has a series of thin dowels running horizontally across so that when the shade is drawn, the fabric is forced into a stack of neat, precise folds (see pages 32 and 33).

Soft Roman shade. The omission of dowels in this means that when the shade is drawn, the fabric spills onto itself in natural folds, which are looser than the classic, strict-looking Roman shade (see page 159).

Balloon shade. A more extreme take on soft Roman shades and a bit fussier, these shades are fuller in width and when gathered, billow with scalloplike folds. When let down, the fullness gathers at the bottom.

curtains

Though simpler in construction than shades and blinds, curtains are the most decorative window treatment of all, offering countless options for customization. Not only can they shield an interior from excess light, but also their ample fabric can keep out drafts and muffle sound. From a design standpoint, a swell of fabric at the windows softens a room's angularity and adds strokes of texture and color.

Traditionally, windows were outfitted in an extravagant three layers of curtain. Glass curtains, also called sash curtains, are sheer scrims made from lightweight fabric that almost cling to the glass, filtering light and bringing a veil of privacy. Then, to block the light, came the unlined draw curtains, which are what we think of as curtain panels today. Finally, purely decorative overdrapery, which is the sometimes static and nonfunctional dressing of the window casement (à la *Amelia Bedelia*). Items like pelmets (that band of fabric-covered wood that conceals the track for draperies) or valances (an elaborate swoop of fabric added over the curtain rod) add to the treatment's formality.

Advice to the modern-day homeowner: Keep the curtains and that's it. An overblown window treatment is like a dowdy skirt-jacket combo. It makes your room look old. Strip away the swoops and swags and you'll be left with windows that are honest, functional, and chic.

REALITY CHECK

THE TERMS CURTAINS,
DRAPERIES, AND THAT AWFUL
NO MAN'S LAND, DRAPES,
ARE USED INTERCHANGEABLY.
CALLING THEM CURTAINS IS
HOW I DISTINGUISH
THE UNFUSSY ROD-HUNG
VARIETY FROM THE
UNATTRACTIVE GATHERED
POLYESTER KIND YOU SEE IN
HOTELS. THE TRUTH IS,
EVEN STATELY ROOMS WITH
EXTRAVAGANT PROPORTIONS
NEED ONLY ELEGANT
CURTAIN PANELS. IN THAT
SCENARIO, THE LUXURY NOTE
COMES FROM THE MATERIAL
(THINK VELVET OR SILK
TAFFETA), THE GENEROUS
AMOUNT OF FABRIC,
AND THE WAY IT IS SIMPLY
SWEPT UP OR LEFT
TO GATHER GRACEFULLY.

typecasting: curtains

There are a myriad of ways that a length of fabric is contorted to create an elaborate curtain. Curtain panels, on the other hand, are simple rectangular sheaths of fabric that gather naturally because the width of the fabric is greater than the span of the window. Instead of asking fabric to perform textile gymnastics under the needle of a sewing machine, curtain panels get their personality from the details: the style of heading or casing (aka the loops or long sleeve at the top of a curtain that the rod slips through), hardware such as rings and tiebacks, and the volume of width and length, which can be adjusted from mellow to majestic. Store-bought curtains (see page 52) offer all these options, and later in the chapter you'll learn how to further customize your curtains and shades.

A cased heading is typically just an extension of the curtain fabric while a tab finish utilizes a contrasting fabric, ribbon, or fabric tape to add interest. In the case of grommets and rings, the hardware should complement either the curtain fabric or the color and finish of the rod on which it's supported.

Curtain Headings

This top border of a curtain, the heading, is where the fabric attaches to the window hardware, letting it open and close with ease.

Cased heading.
This long sleeve covers the supportive rod.

Tab heading.
This heading has flat fabric or ribbon loops that expose the rod.

Eyelet finish.
A professional technique whereby metal grommets as big as bracelets are punched into a fabric, so that it slides easily along the pole.

Wood or metal rings.
These can also be attached to the top of the curtain with curtain hooks, allowing easy maneuvering (see p. 43).

(see p. 43)

Curtain length

The formality of curtains is measured in three standard lengths.

To the windowsill is pretty and neat, with a signature of informality for easygoing rooms and the kitchen, where extra fabric only poses problems. Café curtains, which are generally half the length of a window, can be tiered one on top of the other, or used to cover just the bottom half of a window, which is a perfect solution for letting in a lot of light without sacrificing privacy (see page 25).

To the floor is a graceful treatment that's especially popular in living and dining rooms where it is more desirable to have curtains that barely brush the floor. This makes windows appear longer and a ceiling higher.

Puddling on the floor ratchets up the glamour and romance of a room. Add six to eight inches to the length measurement (rod to floor) so that fabric puddles on the floor.

Curtain width

The horizontal measurement of a curtain panel is what determines fullness, and, in turn, its sumptuousness. It's not enough to have a single panel that barely conceals the window or even two panels that just kiss at the center—most windows crave a bit of fullness. For standard 32- to 36-inch-wide windows, gauge about one and a half times the width of the window for each of the two panels. The excess fabric gathers along the curtain rod when parted, and when closed, there're still dozens of decadent folds.

IF THERE IS ONE THING YOU DO

CLEAN YOUR WINDOWS LIKE THE PROS DO. IT ALWAYS GIVES ROOMS AN EXTRA LITTLE KICK, LIKE TAKING A SIP OF COLD WATER ON A HOT DAY. AND NOTHING WILL LIFT YOUR SPIRITS MORE THAN SPARKLING-CLEAN WINDOWS, INSIDE AND OUT.

• PREPARE A SOLUTION OF WARM WATER AND DISHWASHING DETERGENT.

• DIP A SQUEEGEE IN THE SOAPY SOLUTION AND START AT THE TOP OF A WINDOW (ALWAYS CLEAN TOP TO BOTTOM—YOU WANT GRAVITY TO DO THE WORK FOR YOU) AND PULL THE SQUEEGEE OVER THE GLASS. REPEAT.

• WIPE THE SQUEEGEE'S BLADE CLEAN BETWEEN STROKES WITH A MICROFIBER CLOTH OR CLEAN RAG.

• REMOVE ANY STREAKS FROM THE GLASS WITH A MICROFIBER CLOTH OR CHAMOIS.

• WIPE SILL WITH A RAG.

Curtain hardware

The fittings that help curtains do their job can also be a great source of style.

Spring-tension rods are the easiest and most inexpensive option for mounting a rod inside the window casing. While not a style statement, these rods are meant to be used with cased headings (not tabs or rings), so that the majority of the bar is hidden. Spring-tension rods are available in multiple widths, but are best for average to small windows, because they cannot support more than a few panels of lightweight fabric (see page 25).

Decorative rods can be rendered in metal or wood, or even covered in fabric. Generally, if rings or grommets are used, they should match the color or material of the rod (see opposite page).

Finials are similar to the ornamental lamp pieces that share their name, these decorative end-pieces screw into a freestanding curtain rod to add a bit of interest.

Brackets are wall-mounted supports that carry freestanding curtain rods.

Hold-backs are similar to an elongated doorknob or hook extending from the wall. A hold-back gathers the curtain fabric and pulls it back to reveal the window. A high-mounted hold-back invites more light, while a lower one gives curtains a full feel, but blocks more sun.

Weights such as metal pellets can be sewn inside the hem of a curtain to help fabric drape naturally.

window fabric

The fabric itself sends a message. Sheers and loose-weave cottons lend a carefree, breezy vibe, while soft folds of decadent velvet bring a sumptuous feeling. The fullness of curtains relays a message as does the prim, tailored quality of shades. Though curtains can be made from just about anything that hangs well, there are three standard weights: lightweight, medium-weight, and heavyweight. **Climate and season should be factors in your choice.** While cool seasons can benefit from both a lightweight curtain *and* a more substantial fabric, warmer climes will want to shy away from the heavyweight category.

Lightweight and sheers. These allow a bit of privacy and light filtration, but are typically used in tandem with heavier curtains for more coverage. Thin cotton voile, organdy, and sheer synthetics are common materials.

Medium-weight. Cotton, linen, silk, and taffeta are materials that provide more privacy and light filtration. These are typically lined with lightweight cotton to make them substantial.

Heavyweight. Brocade and velvet are the most significant curtain fabrics and their heft will be a consideration in hanging them. These allow maximum privacy and can also be a deterrent against drafts.

WHY NOT TRY

MAKING A STATEMENT
TO OUTSIDERS:
IF YOU HAVE STREET-LEVEL
CURTAINS, LINE THEM
WITH A BRILLIANT COLOR
OR STRIKING PATTERN
SO THAT PASSERSBY
CAN ENJOY THEM, TOO.

bringing function to fashion

Apart from their assets as decorative icing on the interior design cake, shades and curtains are called on to do more than just look pretty. With the right adjustments, the window dressing you pick for its elegant presence can also do double duty.

Fabric lining is imperative for many curtains because it protects the visible fabric from dust and dirt, encloses raw hems, and adds a bit of weight that helps curtains fall nicely. The main reason to use a lining, though, is to prevent curtain fabric from fading. It also allows for a little sartorial flair. Choose an elegant contrast color for the lining and when it's pushed aside or held back you'll enjoy a vibrant surprise.

Blackout fabric is a necessity for sunny bedrooms and media rooms. It turns even pale-colored shades and curtains into light-fighting heroes. Blackout fabric isn't actually black; it's available in a number of colors and styles, all with a tight weave that keeps errant rays from entering the room.

Insulating fabric should be used in homes in northern climates or older homes with a penchant for drafts. This fabric which has foam, Mylar, or quilted elements, can be attached to the backside of curtains or shades for cozy and energy-saving results. Look for combination blackout-insulating fabric varieties on the market.

tricked out

Just the way a smart black dress can make you look more svelte, there are optical illusions at play in the world of windows. Whether your windows are too low or too squat, too skinny, or just plain misshapen, the way you hang curtains and shades can have an enormous impact on the way you perceive the windows and the room.

To make a window appear taller mount the curtain rod eight inches (instead of the standard four) above the top of the window trim and let the curtain fall from the rod to the floor. For a shade, mount it above the window casement so that when the shade is fully pulled up, the bottom border covers just the very top of the glass, therefore hiding the casement window frame's exact location.

To make a window appear wider mount curtain-rod brackets four inches above the window molding and at least five inches to either side of it, equidistant from the window, and add a curtain rod that spans the distance. Consider your new measurement (say, 46 inches wide, instead of 36) as the width of your window. Buy two curtain panels, each the width of your new measurement. When open, the curtains should be slid along the rail to overlap the window molding, revealing only glass and tricking the eye into thinking the window extends behind the curtain, beyond what is visible. For a Roman shade, purchase one that covers the molding, plus a few inches on either side.

To downplay an overpowering window such as sliding glass doors, a bay window, or a plate-glass wall, mount one rod across the top of the molding and hang several curtain panels (that are as wide as possible), to break up the expanse.

LIGHTBULB

DON'T OVERLOOK HOW YOUR WINDOW FUNCTIONS. YOUR PREFERRED COVERING SHOULDN'T INTERFERE WITH HOW YOUR WINDOW OPENS AND CLOSES. FOR EXAMPLE, VERTICAL SHADES MAY NOT BE THE IDEAL CHOICE FOR A WINDOW THAT OPENS HORIZONTALLY.

To disguise a poor view mount a sheer scrim inside the window casement, hanging close to the glass. Use one panel instead of two (which might tempt guests to part them). Measure the width of the window itself and multiply by one and a half for a standard amount of fullness, or to two times for a richer look. Add curtains or shades, mounted traditionally. The scrim can be static while the additional window coverings can be used to control light. For a more modern take, try sewing two dowels at the top and bottom of a panel of voile or muslin, and hang it taut in the window casement.

To block the maximum amount of light for rooms with valuable art and for rooms with bright light that can fade upholstery, a curtain rod mounted six inches above the molding and extending at least three inches beyond the window's width on each side is recommended. This generous proportion will envelop the area so that no errant light escapes.

what's in store: off-the-rack shades and curtains

Making curtains yourself requires just a bit of labor, but it's likely that you'll have already hung and parted the store-bought variety by the time you've warmed up your sewing machine.

The market is packed with ingenious ready-to-hang varieties of shades and curtains and all you need to make them look tailor-made is a tape measure and a bit of know-how.

Taking **exact measurements is key.** To do so, use a metal measuring tape and record dimensions to an eighth of an inch. Measure every window in your home because looks are deceiving: A pair of windows in the living room may not be identical. It's helpful to take several measurements of the same dimension. Width, for example, should be measured at the top, middle, and sill-level. For shades, buy them according to the smallest measurement; for curtains, the largest. And if you're buying for several rooms at once, clearly mark which dimensions relate to which room so you won't get confused when you're pondering color and pattern choices. The following measuring details will help with finding specific window treatments.

how to measure for curtains

1. **Curtain length** depends on where the curtain is mounted and how far it will fall. For an inside mount, measure inside the window casement; for trim mounts, measure from the top of the molding; for wall mounts, start from four inches above the molding (where the rod will be). Then measure to the sill or the floor. If you'd like your curtain to pool on the floor, add six to eight inches to the floor measurement. If you're using one of the tricks to change a window's appearance (see page 46), adjust the trim size accordingly.

2. **Curtain fullness** depends on the width of your panels and how many panels you use. Take the width of the window and use the following formulas. For a neat, tailored look, use the exact width measurement plus two inches; for a traditional look, multiply the measurement by one and a half; for a sumptuous, gathered look, multiply by three. This measurement applies to the total width of the panels, which means you can buy a panel that spans the whole width, or break it into two, three, or four panels or more.

3. **Curtain panels** come in a variety of widths, but 42 and 50 inches are standard. Curtain lengths are in increments such as 36, 45, 63, 72, 81, 84, 90, 96, and 108 inches. If you find the right length, look for curtains with a hem that's at least four inches, which will help it fall naturally. When in doubt, buy curtains that are longer or wider than you need; hemming is cheap and easy. And if you live in a city and have windows exposed to exhaust or smog, consider opting for a curtain made from washable fabric, such as cotton, which will be more affordable than dry cleaning.

4. **Curtain rods** run the width of the window. Measure the width of the window molding. Add one to three inches on each side of the window to leave room for the curtains to gather (or more or less if you're using a trick, see page 46). Leave room for decorative finials, if desired; that length is not factored into the rod measurement.

EDUCATED CONSUMER

IF YOU HAVE ODD-SIZED WINDOWS OR IF READY-MADE CURTAINS DON'T SUIT YOUR STYLE, YOU'LL PROBABLY WANT TO VISIT A PROFESSIONAL SEAMSTRESS FOR CUSTOM SHADES OR CURTAINS. BEFORE YOU MAKE AN APPOINTMENT, ARM YOURSELF WITH THE RIGHT INFO. YOU'LL NEED MEASUREMENTS OF YOUR WINDOWS INCLUDING THE MOLDING OR TRIM, INSIDE THE CASEMENT, AND DEPTH FROM THE GLASS TO THE OUTER EDGE OF THE MOLDING OR CASEMENT; DIGITAL PHOTOS OF THE WHOLE ROOM AND WINDOW DETAILS WILL HELP IMMENSELY. KNOW WHETHER YOU WANT A TREATMENT DONE AS AN INSIDE OR OUTSIDE MOUNT AND IF YOU WANT THEM LINED OR UNLINED. THE MORE CLEARLY YOU CAN EXPLAIN YOUR VISION, THE HAPPIER YOU'LL BE WITH THE RESULTS.

how to measure for shades

For Roman shades, first decide if you'd like an inside mount (where the shade is tucked inside the window casement) or an outside mount (where the shade is mounted above the window casement). Common widths for Roman shades are 26, 32, 36, 44, 48, and 58. A common length is 63 inches.

Inside mount
A neat look that suits modern or formal interiors or windows that have architecturally nice moldings.

1. Measure the width and length of the window opening.

2. Measure the depth of the window; make sure that the mounting board and the stacked material of the shade will fit comfortably between the glass and the outer edge of the trim. The depth of the drawn shade is approximately 15 to 20 percent of the shade length.

Outside mount
This style can make a window appear larger, by hiding its trim; it can also disguise less-than-beautiful moldings.

1. Measure the width of the window trim. Add the number of inches overlap you desire—the more width overlap, the less light escapes and the more privacy.

2. For length, start your measurement around four inches above the window trim, where you'll hang the mounting board. Measure from that spot to the windowsill or farther for longer-looking windows.

upgrading store-bought curtains and shades

You can get a customized look from off-the-shelf curtains and shades by adding some dressmaker details, like trim and hardware. Here are a few of the most effective tricks of the trade.

Block Party: A perfect way to turn too-short curtains into a style statement. Add a panel of fabric or decorative scallop or sicles to the bottom and/or of a ready-made curtain or shade (see opposite, left). And have fun with mixing textures; if your curtain is silk, add velvet or attach a sheer fabric to linen. All it takes is a straight stitch on the sewing machine, but it's also just an hour-long job for any tailor.

Trim Fit: Grosgrain ribbon, fabric trim, or twill tape can add a chic decorative border when stitched to curtains or shades. For a pair of curtains, try a patterned trim running along the inner and bottom edges to create "L's or loops of style (see opposite, right). On shades, attach a border of twill tape about two inches from the perimeter and all the way around the panel for a neat, tailored look.

Layer It On: Don't stop at just two panels, but layer the window with sheers and curtains or shades and curtains, to give the treatment a little more depth. The first layer can have an inner mount (such as on a tension rod) and the second, outer.

Accessorize: Adding new hardware can bring lackluster curtains back to life. Curtain rods in one of dozens of finishes and finials in a myriad of styles can bring a note of architecture to curtains that were previously hung simply like with tension rods (see page 42). Hardware like hold-backs offer a bit of wall jewelry.

CHAPTER 3

living room

in this chapter you will learn:
how to choose a sofa that lasts
how to pick chairs, coffee tables, occasional tables, and lighting
how to lay out a room
how to accessorize a room
how to style a side table

IF
SOMEONE
ASKED
ME
TO PICK
A FAVORITE
ROOM
IN MY
HOME,
I'D HAVE
TO DECLARE
THE
LIVING ROOM
THE WINNER.

While I love everything about my living room, I'm most passionate about its chairs. Chairs are my favorite type of furniture because they come in all shapes and sizes and are full of personality, just like people, which would explain why I'm never lonely in this space, even when no one else is home. I own chairs of every possible kind: Swedish barrel-back chairs that curve around me like a hug, sprightly curlicue-backed French metal chairs, a George III low-slung, high-backed armchair that is great for reading in, and an Aesthetic Movement armchair that makes me sit up as straight as an arrow. I didn't buy any of them with a real decorating plan in mind; instead I bought them purely based on love. If you learn only one lesson from this book, be it that you **buy only what you love.**

That may seem like a no-brainer but it's easy to make compromises when you're shopping. Maybe you love the shape of a sofa but not its color or you run across a carpet that's a bit small for the room but it has a price tag you can't resist. But do try to resist! The closer you come to loving every single thing about every object in your home, the more consistent the style of your home will be. You probably don't define your taste with a simple term like French Country or Global Bohemian, but you know what you love. There's a vision in that alone. **Follow your gut and buy what you're crazy about and you'll see the style called "You" emerge.**

My living room sofa was a decadent splurge but well worth it. Unlike chairs, which are portable and fit easily into any room, the sofa acts as an anchor; it dictates the scale of the other furniture in the room.

I had this particular one custom-made to look like a sofa I once saw at a photo shoot when I was decorating editor at *House Beautiful*. I opted to cover it in deep pink silk velvet (which was inspired by a hue found in my favorite printed pillow). When it finally arrived months later I showed it to my husband, whose reaction was, "It's pink!" Yes, but solid pink, I explained, because if you **cover a sofa in solid-colored fabric, you'll never be married to just one style** (like you might be if you opted for a floral). To temper the sofa's girliness I peppered the room with lots of chocolate brown.

The curtains for this room were inspired by the style of a gray skirt worn by a fellow editor. It fell straight to midthigh with an attached pleated border continuing to just above the knee. I snapped a picture of it as the editor sat in my office and I knew right away I'd have curtains made to mimic the style of the skirt. I still have the photograph in my decorating file. The best way to get a sense of what you love is to **keep a file of inspiring photos, tear sheets, and swatches.** That way you'll always have your best ideas at the ready.

While the living room comfortably seats ten people, it doesn't seem overcrowded. A circular ottoman is vital to this plan because it provides an extra perch without taking up visual clutter like another pair of chairs would. It also adds a much-needed rounded edge. I was very conscious of shape when I shopped for my coffee table and occasional tables, too. One is round, another thin and narrow, and the other low and rectangular. **Vary the shapes of furniture and objects to keep a room visually interesting.** Similarly, keep height in mind. Willowy pieces carry your eye up, and break up the low horizon of a room. In an antiques store in upstate New York, I stumbled upon a very tall but slim French secretary, which was the perfect fit for the wall space between my living room's two windows (see page vi). I was drawn to its elegant proportions and its tiny divided shelves, which are perfect for storing stationery (the antiques dealer claims that it used to be in a French post office). Now it's the most commented-on piece in my living room; in a sea of low tables and seating, its stature commands attention. **Every room needs a tall piece of furniture.** And though too many tall pieces can come off as formal or grand, a few sprinkled in among smaller-scale pieces will feel cozy and enveloping, just like your favorite chair.

sofas

The sofa is the living room's leading lady. Without her, the show cannot go on. Generally speaking, the larger and more permanent a piece of furniture, the greater its impact on a room, which is what makes the living room the Sofa Show. But don't be tempted to buy one so ginormous that it's the proverbial elephant in the room; it **should take up between 1/3 to 1/2 of a wall and no more**. Its depth and height count, too. A sofa's overall volume should be proportionate to the room; if it is too big, your room will feel off-kilter and you'll never feel fully at ease there. Take cues from your living room architecture: the grander the space, the larger you can go with your sofa. A generous modern sectional better suits a vast space with soaring ceilings than it would the petite rooms of an historic home.

TEST DRIVE

IMAGINING WHAT THE SHOWROOM-MODEL SOFA WILL LOOK LIKE IN YOUR LIVING ROOM IS NEXT TO IMPOSSIBLE UNLESS YOU'RE SPATIALLY GIFTED. TO GET A SENSE OF ITS FOOTPRINT, TAKE ITS LENGTH AND WIDTH MEASUREMENTS AT THE STORE (OR CRIB THEM FROM THE ONLINE SPEC SHEET) AND AT HOME, CUT OUT A SAME-SIZE KRAFT-PAPER PATTERN. IF IT'S TOO BIG OR SMALL, ALTER THIS PAPER "SOFA" TO FIT YOUR SPACE, AND THEN SHOP FOR ONE THAT MATCHES YOUR SPECIFICATIONS.

IF THERE'S ONE THING YOU DO

AVOID DISASTER. THE HYSTERICAL STORY ABOUT THE SOFA THAT DIDN'T FIT THROUGH THE DOOR (AND HAD TO BE SAWED IN HALF AND THEN REASSEMBLED) IS ONLY FUNNY WHEN IT HAPPENS TO SOMEONE ELSE. TAKE MEASUREMENTS OF DOORWAYS, STAIRWAYS, AND ANYWHERE THERE'S A TIGHT SQUEEZE. PROVIDE THE SHOP OR SHOWROOM WITH THE MEASUREMENTS AND ASK THEM TO CONFIRM THAT THE PIECE WILL FIT, AND THAT IF IT DOESN'T YOU CAN RETURN IT.

typecasting: sofas

When you first set out to create your living room, you may not have a crystal-clear vision of how you want it to look when it is completely furnished. So which sofa do you pick if you're unsure of your decor? Buy one of these three tried-and-true shapes that will accommodate as many situations and styles as you can get yourself into.

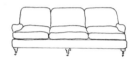

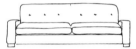

Traditional. Typified by curvy lines and old-fashioned details such as tufting, pleating, or a skirt. The camelback, named for its arched, upholstered seat back and Bridgewater-style sofas, which have thick, taut cushions, are classics. A button-tufted Chesterfield and a boxy English Knole have arms as high as their backs making them somewhat formal feeling, but enveloping.

Modern. Strict, clean lines and a boxy shape define these sofas. Many are low to the ground, making them informal and unfussy, but still provide a sense of architecture and order. Most sectional sofas adhere to modern lines.

Armless. For a small space, this offers maximum seating using minimal room. Though they usually have a modern silhouette, these sofas can be intricately upholstered, making them adaptable to any decor.

EDUCATED CONSUMER

BE WARY OF SOFAS THAT ARE LARGE ENOUGH TO FIT THREE OR FOUR PEOPLE BUT HAVE ONLY TWO SEAT CUSHIONS. NO ONE EVER WANTS TO SIT ON THE "CRACK," SO USUALLY ONLY TWO PEOPLE END UP ON THE SOFA. INSTEAD, SEEK A SOFA WITH ONE LONG CUSHION OR SEVERAL SQUARE CUSHIONS THAT PROVIDE A DEFINED SPOT FOR EVERY GUEST.

PANIC BUTTON

BUY A TRADITIONAL, CAMELBACK SOFA BECAUSE YOU CAN NEVER GO WRONG WITH A CLASSIC SHAPE AND YOU CAN BRING IT UP-TO-DATE WITH MODERN PILLOWS AND TEXTILES.

IF THERE'S ONE THING YOU DO

WHEN CHOOSING SOFA
FABRICS, APPLY THE SAME
WISDOM YOU WOULD WHILE
CLOTHES SHOPPING.
THAT MEANS THAT EVEN IF
YOU'RE MAD FOR PLAID THIS
SEASON, IT'S IN YOUR BEST
INTEREST TO BEELINE
TOWARD A SOLID COLOR. A
KICKY PRINT OR BOLD FLORAL
WILL ONLY LIMIT YOUR
DECORATING OPTIONS BUT A
SOLID-COLOR SOFA WON'T
HINDER YOUR ROOM FROM
EVOLVING. THAT'S BECAUSE IT
CAN BE PAIRED EASILY
WITH ANY NUMBER OF
ACCESSORIES (OR WALL
PAINT, FOR THAT MATTER).
[READ MORE ABOUT
UPHOLSTERY FABRIC IN THE
FAMILY ROOM, PAGE 164.]

know your stuff

It's what's inside that counts. Sofa shape is vital to the overall style of the room, but it's the stuffing that determines comfort level. [For more on comfort, see Family Room page 163.] The idea of sinking into a deep, cushy pile of down is delightful, but a sofa that looks like an unmade bed is not. Tight-back cushions, which maintain their shape even without constant fluffing, are an all-purpose favorite.

Pillow fillings depend on the style of your sofa. If it's tightly tailored, a firmer filling is needed. Styles with lots of tucking and draping and soft, loose cushions use a fluffier filling. Down is pricey and squishy, down-covered foam is better, while shredded foam loses shape quickly.

Down is a type of goose feather and is the most expensive filling and the most luxurious. It can be used alone for accent pillows, and in combination with other fibers for seat cushions.

Fluffy polyester comes in rolls of varying thicknesses. It can be used by itself or as a wrapping for polyurethane foam. It provides smooth, rounded, and soft cushions.

Polyurethane foam is a popular and reliable material that excels at shaping and stuffing and comes in degrees of firmness from Soft, Medium, Super Resilient (SR), Firm, Extra Firm, and High Resiliency (HR) for the most firm. Newer foams belonging to the High Resilience (HR) family offer a soft initial feel and then firm up as more pressure is put on it, yielding very comfortable and supportive seating.

Hair blends is the firmest of all fills and guarantees a long life. Horsehair was the material used in Victorian-era sofas, making them rather stiff and unyielding. Today, hair filling, usually hog hair or cattle hair mixed with other fibers, is more flexible and inviting, with better resilience and plenty of comfort and bounce.

construction zone

Stuffing is one indicator of quality, but be prepared to ask a showroom rep a few questions about sofa construction, too, which is the basis for its longevity. **Four things to investigate:**

Frames that are kiln-dried hardwoods such as maple are the strongest. Legs that are part of the frame are more durable than ones screwed in.

Springs should be eight-way, hand-tied steel—the strongest, most resilient, most flexible, and longest-lasting construction available. With this technique, springs are tied together in eight directions so that all the coils work in unison. Upholstered furniture of lesser quality may secure its springs with only four ties, which will eventually cause the springs to separate and create lumpiness. The number of springs is also an indicator of quality, with 12 springs being the highest standard per seat section (i.e., the space that one cushion or one guest occupies) and six on the low end. Invest in the highest quality sofa you can afford and you'll never have to scour the market again.

Upholstery featuring patterns and trim should be aligned; zippers should match the fabric hue and should be covered with fabric. If the sofa has a skirt, it should be lined and weighted.

Comfort is of the utmost importance. After your sit test, squeeze the arm and back to make sure you don't feel anything hard (which would mean too little padding) and try to lift a corner of the sofa. Struggling is a good sign—quality sofas are heavy.

LIGHTBULB

IF YOU PICK A NEUTRAL COLOR—BEIGE, TAN, SAND, HONEY, OCHRE—FOR FURNITURE, FLOORS, AND WALLS, YOU'LL BE ABLE TO ADAPT THE ROOM'S STYLE WITH ACCESSORIES AND ART MORE EASILY IN THE FUTURE.

rugs

If you think of the living room as a collage of furniture, then consider the rug as the glue uniting the sofa, chairs, and tables. Homes with a "great room" instead of finite living and dining spaces will find an area rug especially practical because its boundaries help define an intimate room within a larger box. [See more about carpets in Family Room, page 158.]

Area rugs are a commitment-free accessory perfect for those who update their surroundings with the seasons. Simply roll up and store a wool Berber when it comes time for summery sisal. A fancy floor covering, however, can be a quick way to blow your budget. A rug should provide comfort, muffle sound, and act as a canvas for furniture. An inexpensive model can do this just as well as a bank-breaking one. Why draw attention to the floor when there are so many more rewarding elements of the room to play with?

MEASURE FOR MEASURE

FOR AREA RUGS THAT
CONSUME THE MAJORITY OF
THE FLOOR SPACE, LEAVE AT
LEAST A SIX-INCH PERIMETER
BETWEEN THE WALL AND
THE CARPET TO GIVE IT ROOM
TO BREATHE.

TEST DRIVE

WHEN YOU'RE SOLD ON
A RUG, ASK TO BUY IT ON A
LOAN BASIS. MANY
REPUTABLE SHOWROOMS
WILL ALLOW YOU TO TAKE
A RUG HOME AND
TRY IT AMONG YOUR
FURNISHINGS BEFORE YOU
COMMIT FOR GOOD.

typecasting: rugs

What you choose for a rug's size, shape, and material should be influenced by the room's decor, but a moderately priced carpet in a neutral palette is a good bet.

Solid vs. Pattern. A solid-color rug is hands down the safest pick. But many patterns, especially in neutral or earthy colors, are just as agreeable. One benefit of picking a pattern or texture: Dirt or stains aren't immediately obvious. If you choose an ostentatious pattern, the rug becomes the focal point for which you make all your design choices: upholstery, curtains, and accessories. When coordinating prints, start here (for more on prints, see Family Room, page 170).

Color. Whites and pastels won't mask spills and stains and deep colors reveal every stray thread and speck of lint. Avoid extremes and pick a happy medium.

Shape and Size. A square or rectangle is the most logical shape for a room, but a circular rug adds diversity. In many rooms, an 8 x 10-foot rug is large enough to get furniture (at least two legs) on top of the setting. Smaller versions can be used to delineate part of a seating arrangement. Common sizes for new rugs are 2' x 3', 4' x 6', 5' x 8', 6' x 9', and 8' x 10', though antique and ethnic varieties don't adhere to that, and tend to run on the smaller side.

LIGHTBULB

TO INCREASE THE LIFE OF
YOUR RUG, KEEP IT CLEAN SO
THAT DIRT DOESN'T ERODE
ITS FIBERS. VACUUM BOTH
SIDES AND USE A RUG PAD TO
PROTECT THE UNDERSIDE.

EDUCATED CONSUMER

TO TELL IF THE RUG YOU'RE
LOOKING AT IS HANDMADE,
SPREAD APART ITS PILE.
IF YOU SEE KNOTS AT THE
BASE OF THE FIBERS, THE RUG
IS MADE BY HAND.

material matters

The types of fibers in your rug will dictate its style, but mostly its longevity. Wool and wool blends are long lasting, while cotton and natural fibers signal an unfussy, warm-weather feeling.

Cotton is commonly used in flat-weave rugs. It offers a light, summery look. It's inexpensive and relatively cheap to have professionally cleaned, and small sizes can be machine-washed and air-dried. While it's not ultradurable, its reasonable price makes up for it. Antique Turkish kilim rugs are usually made of cotton and/or hemp.

Wool is by far the hardiest material, hence the plethora of antique varieties. The lanolin in wool naturally resists stains. Both tufted Oriental rugs and fuzzy flokati rugs fall in this category.

Natural fibers such as sisal and sea grass mats originally replaced wool rugs in the summer months, but they've turned into a professional decorator's favorite because their neutral background complements so many styles. Unfortunately, natural fibers have short life spans, are difficult to clean, and are ultimately disposable.

REALITY CHECK

HERE'S THE TRUTH ABOUT SISAL: IT'S NOT COMFORTABLE. ON PAPER, IT'S LOVELY, AND IT APPEARS CONSTANTLY IN MAGAZINES AND CATALOGS BECAUSE IT'S NEUTRAL AND TEXTURED, MAKING IT AN IDEAL CANVAS FOR FURNITURE. BUT IF YOU CRAVE SOMETHING SOFT UNDERFOOT, STEP AWAY FROM THIS PRICKLY FLOOR COVERING.

getting grounded

To make an intimate seating area, arrange all your furniture within the confines of the rug. Or, if you're working with a small rug, place just the coffee table and the front legs of most of the furniture on it. **When arranging furniture in tandem with a rug, think of the rug as a stage.** Most of the furniture in the room should be in the spotlight. The coffee table always takes center stage, so when you first lay down the rug, center the coffee table at the midpoint of the rug's length.

The placement of the rest of the furniture depends on the size of the rug. If it's 8' x 10' or larger, then try to place the legs of most of the furniture within its boundaries. Otherwise, position at least the front two legs of the sofa and chairs at least three inches inside the rug perimeter. Nearly every piece of furniture in the primary seating arrangement (sofa, two chairs, and coffee table) should be placed on a piece of the rug. Inevitably there will be furniture that isn't on the carpet: side tables, a hutch or desk against the wall, or a pair of side chairs flanking a door. It will look most natural if there are several pieces in that scenario, not just one lone table and lamp off in a corner.

coffee tables

With so many seats orbiting around it, the coffee table is the natural center of the living room universe. Not just a receptacle for drinks and books, the coffee table often steps up to host full-on dinners when the occasion doesn't necessitate the dining room. **The materials of the coffee table go a long way in solidifying—or softening—a room's look.** If the sitting area already feels very grounded with substantial furniture and a pleasing layout, find a way to introduce lightness. One way is with a bit of gloss. Metals, laminates, glass, and acrylic all bring a glint of light into the center of the room. Or, choose a wood model frame that is sinuous, not blocky.

There's a fine line between a table that's at everyone's fingertips and one that's a roadblock. A gap of around 18 inches between a seat and the table is the sweet spot. But beware sharp edges—glass and metal versions are especially likely to have gash-inducing corners.

PANIC BUTTON

IF YOU'RE IN A COMPLETE
QUANDARY AS TO WHICH
COFFEE TABLE TO BUY,
CHOOSE A SIMPLE
RECTANGULAR ACRYLIC
VERSION (SEE PHOTOGRAPH
OPPOSITE PAGE). THIS
ALL-PURPOSE SHAPE WILL
COMPLEMENT MOST SOFAS
AND ITS CLEAR BODY
DOESN'T TAKE UP ANY
VISUAL WEIGHT. IT
PRACTICALLY DISAPPEARS
INTO THE ROOMSCAPE.

typecasting: coffee tables

To determine a style and material for your coffee table, look first at your sofa and then find a contrasting, but complementary look. If it's dark-colored, go light; if it's a very substantial sofa, such as one with thick blocklike legs, try lightening the mood with a delicate metal table. Conversely, if you can easily see the lithe legs of your sofa, find a coffee table with a bit of heft.

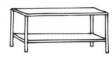

Rectangle. The most popular style because it is a natural fit in a seating scheme. The more narrow the table width, the more intimate your seating arrangement.

Nesting. A pair or three tables that fit inside each other. They're easy to maneuver (you can lift most with one hand) and are a terrific space saver. Using two side by side as an alternative to a rectangular table brings varied heights into a typically flat area.

Round. Space efficient it's not, but a circular table brings a cozy vibe to the center of the room by breaking up a space that's usually gridlocked by rectangles.

MEASURE FOR MEASURE

COFFEE TABLES SHOULD BE
OF SIMILAR HEIGHT TO SOFA
AND CHAIR CUSHIONS WHEN
YOU'RE SITTING (MEANING
A BIT SQUISHED), SO AROUND
17 INCHES HIGH. GENERALLY,
THE LENGTH OF A
RECTANGULAR TABLE, OR
DIAMETER OF A ROUND,
SHOULD BE ABOUT HALF THE
LENGTH OF THE SOFA.

WHY NOT TRY

AN OTTOMAN INSTEAD OF A
COFFEE TABLE? WITH A
LARGE TRAY ON TOP FOR
BOOKS AND BEVERAGES, IT'S
A SURFACE FOR EVERYDAY
USE, AND WITHOUT ONE, IT'S
AN EXTRA PLACE FOR A PAIR
OF PEOPLE TO PERCH. PICK
AN OTTOMAN IN ANY SHAPE
BUT MAKE SURE IT'S NO
TALLER THAN THE SOFA'S
SEAT. [FOR MORE ON
OTTOMANS, SEE PAGE 172.]

occasional tables

With a coffee table in place, you've nailed down the most essential surface in the room, but don't stop there. Occasional tables, including a pair to bookend the sofa, are essential, too, if only to hold table lamps.

Instead of choosing a matching set of surfaces, pick a few different styles to add wit to the room. Mixing shapes is a good way to start. A circular side table will fill the gap between a sofa and adjacent chair. A large rectangle will hold a lamp, books or objects, plus beverages, effectively tripling its usage. Occasional tables are meant to be convenient, so make sure they're not a struggle to reach. Measure the table against the arm of the nearest sofa or chair; it should stand no lower than two inches below the nearest arm.

Snack tables and drink tables are charismatic additions to a living room and can be pulled from the sidelines for an occasion. Named so because they don't hold much more than a cocktail or nibble, these tables are frequently pedestal-style and light as a feather.

typecasting : occasional tables

Have a bit of fun when picking occasional tables. Try to use materials not seen in the rest of the room such as acrylic or lacquer for a modern effect or a wood piece with an elegant marble top for a more traditional approach.

Round. Adding a circle to the living room mix breaks up the inevitable gridlock of a room full of rectangles.

Rectagular. Squares and rectangles can fit seamlessly against other furniture in the room, so look for a style that has a generous enough surface to hold a lamp or a drawer for covert storage.

Pedestal. A single-leg table that fans out at the base and surface is a swanlike presence in the face of more blocky furnishings.

Nesting. The tallest member in a pair or triplet of these tables is appropriate as a stationary side table while the smaller ones can be pulled out as needed.

WHY NOT TRY

USING A LOW CHEST AS A
SIDE TABLE SO THAT YOUR
STORAGE SOLUTIONS DOUBLE
AS YOUR TABLETOP. IF YOUR
SOFA IS FLOATING, ADD A
SOFA TABLE, CREDENZA, OR
LOW BOOKSHELF BEHIND IT
SO THAT THE TABLETOP IS
FLUSH WITH THE TOP OF THE
SOFA OR A BIT LOWER.

chairs

Chairs' ability to add instant personality to a room is unrivaled by other furnishings. They quickly send a message to your guests about what kind of space your living room is. Tall upright seats with tight cushions evoke a feeling of formality whereas low-slung furniture, especially with ample padding, gives a more laid-back lounge vibe. Just like a party guest list, a mix of personalities is crucial. At least one chair, such as a club chair, should be out-and-out indulgent. Others should contribute wit or whimsy with unusual shapes, such as fanciful scrolling ironwork or cartoonish mid-century curves.

Each chair in the main seating area should be within arm's reach of a coffee table or side table. A traditional arrangement puts one seat to each side of the sofa. This provides two natural conversation nooks (or one large one) and makes the room symmetrical. But not every chair in the living room should be on the front lines. Nominate one pair to be wallflowers, ready to be pulled into action when the occasion strikes.

typecasting: chairs

Even a small room can fit a pair of chairs while large spaces, with multiple seating areas, might make room for half a dozen or more. Remember that low chairs and those with open arms or backs lessen the visual impact, which can make a small room look bigger.

Club chair. This comfortable classic has an upholstered body and arms and a single seat and back cushion (which can be attached or not). Typically, it has a boxy shape, so avoid this style if you have a sectional sofa, which would be overkill.

Side chair. This armless, easy-to-move straight-back seat overlaps styles with the dining room (see page 124). It can have an upholstered seat or not, but generally has exposed legs, making it elegant and airy and a good pick to flank a sofa. For small spaces, look for seat backs that allow light to pass through.

Wingback. An armchair with a shapely, exaggerated seat back that extends above and around the head of the seat. The upholstered chair is often seen in leather, which gives it a gentleman's-library feel.

Barrel back. A solid, rounded back encases the seat; models with a small stature are more graceful than larger ones.

Armless or slipper. A key chair for small spaces, this generously upholstered chair offers comfort without bulk. For maximum convenience, look for legs with casters, which makes even the most substantial chairs mobile.

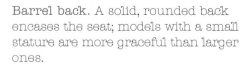

REMEMBER THAT FURNITURE AND ACCESSORIES IN YOUR HOME REFLECT YOUR PERSONALITY, BUT THEY CAN ALSO SEND MESSAGES TO VISITORS AND HOUSE GUESTS. LIVING ROOM CHAIRS ARE A GOOD EXAMPLE; DEPENDING ON YOUR CHOICE, YOU CAN DRAMATICALLY TEMPER THE MOOD OF A ROOM. A PAIR OF TRADITIONAL STRAIGHT-BACK CHAIRS OR A TIGHTLY UPHOLSTERED SET BRING AN ELEMENT OF FORMALITY THAT CALLS FOR QUICK VISITS ONLY — TOO LONG AND YOUR GUESTS WILL BEGIN SHIFTING IN THEIR SEAT UNCOMFORTABLY. A MORE RELAXED STYLE, SUCH AS CLUB CHAIRS AND OVER-STUFFED SEATS SEND THE MESSAGE: "STAY AWHILE." INVITING GUESTS TO GET COMFY AND SLOUCH A BIT, ESPECIALLY WHEN COUPLED WITH AN OTTOMAN FOR KICKING UP HEELS.

furniture arrangements

Once you've added chairs to the mix, step back and see if it works. Ask yourself a few questions: Does it look good? Does it seem balanced where nothing overwhelms the room? Is there a surface within reach of most chairs? When you sit on the sofa, do you have a nice view?

Then, put it into action. **The easiest way to test your setup is by hosting a get-together (which also happens to be the most fun method).** There's wisdom in groups, so keep an eye on your guests; you'll learn a lot by watching them interact with the room. Are they sitting comfortably or constantly rearranging themselves? Do they move nimbly around furniture or do they have to move things aside? Does anyone scoot a chair out of its place—perhaps to better talk with someone, or to reach a table? Take stock and then make adjustments for comfort.

WHY NOT TRY

CREATING A FOCAL POINT
OPPOSITE YOUR SOFA IF YOU
DON'T ALREADY HAVE
A NATURAL ONE, SUCH AS A
FIREPLACE OR A WINDOW.
HANG AN EYE-CATCHING
PIECE OF ART OR MIRROR
OVER A CONSOLE TABLE AS
AN ALTERNATIVE.

typecasting: furniture arrangements

The tenets of room design hold true whether your room is tiny or grand. Start with the first illustration below and add furniture as space allows.

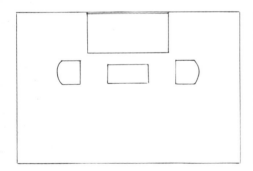

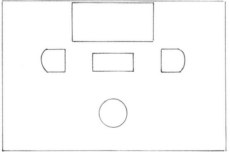

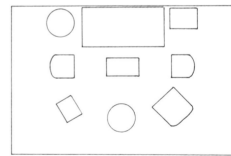

One sofa, two chairs, and coffee table. The quintessential room layout. It's well balanced, maneuverable, and welcoming. A classic in any size room.

One sofa, two chairs, coffee table, and an ottoman. An ottoman adds comfort and extra seating without cluttering the room.

One sofa, two side tables, two chairs, coffee table, ottoman, and two more chairs. The last pair of chairs can be offset as part of the main seating area (in their own conversation nook), against a wall, flanking a doorway, floating in a corner, or at a desk until they're pulled into action.

MEASURE FOR MEASURE

EIGHTEEN INCHES IS THE
MINIMUM SPACE FOR A
PASSAGEWAY, BUT EVERY
ROOM SHOULD HAVE TWO
CLEAR FOOTPATHS THAT ARE
A FEW FEET WIDE OR
LARGER.

IF THERE'S ONE THING YOU DO

KEEP YOUR FURNITURE
SQUARED OFF IN THE ROOM'S
CORNERS. THERE'S SOME-
THING UNSETTLING ABOUT
POSING FURNITURE AT AN
ANGLE BECAUSE IT DOESN'T
ALIGN WITH THE GEOMETRY
OF THE ROOM, IT CREATES AN
AWKWARD ANGLE, AND—
EVEN WORSE—IT GIVES THE
FEELING THAT YOU'RE HIDING
SOMETHING.

lighting

Living room lighting comes in three forms: ambient, task, and accent. Ambient lighting from table or floor lamps is simply a stand-in for sunlight; it illuminates the room in a general way. Task lighting is focused, such as for reading; while accent (or mood) lighting is purely decorative.

Forget central overhead fixtures in the living room altogether—the light they cast is harsh and unflattering. Instead, opt for several points of light scattered around the room. **Use a mix of standing and table lamps.** Built-in lighting, like spotlights or track lighting, are ideal for highlighting art, but shouldn't be a primary source.

In the evening, take it down a notch. Dimmers, which can be clipped into a standard outlet, give you the most control. Dial it back from the strongest light, but leave on enough glow to avoid a sleepy room.

IF THERE'S ONE THING YOU DO

INSTALL A CFL (COMPACT
FLUORESCENT LIGHT). THEY
SAVE 75 TO 80 PERCENT MORE
ENERGY THAN STANDARD
BULBS, AND LAST UP TO 20
TIMES LONGER. IF EVERY
HOUSEHOLD IN AMERICA
USED JUST ONE CFL BULB IN
PLACE OF A 60-WATT BULB,
THE ENERGY SAVED WOULD
BE ENOUGH TO POWER A CITY
OF 1.5 MILLION PEOPLE
(THAT'S D.C. AND MARYLAND
COMBINED). THE COLOR AND
QUALITY OF CFLS ARE
GETTING MORE AGREEABLE
EACH DAY, BUT IF THE LIGHT
FEELS HARSH TO YOU, USE
THEM IN TRANSITIONAL SPOTS
LIKE AN ENTRYWAY, FOYER,
HALLWAY, OR FOR AN
OUTSIDE FIXTURE THAT STAYS
ON ALL NIGHT.

typecasting: lighting

Use a mix of lamp styles and try to balance where the light is centered. To avoid too much symmetry (such as a light in every corner), position lighting to create a triangular blanket of light throughout the room.

Table lamps. Place these on side tables near seating, with lampshades hovering on the same plane as the head of someone seated. Use 75- to 100-watt bulbs where you plan to read.

Floor lamps. A standard version is five feet tall, but use a taller model for a room with high ceilings. These add a bit of interest to an empty corner, but are also a neat way to light a single seat. If you can see the bulb from anywhere in the room, use 60 watts or less to soften the effect.

Spotlights. Low wattage small spots and library lights, which are usually recessed in the ceiling or on tracks, are effective in lighting bookcases, art, objects, and dark spots. Try clip-on styles if your bookcases aren't wired for picture lights.

WHY NOT TRY

ADDING A PAIR OF SCONCES
ABOVE THE SOFA OR
FLANKING A DOORWAY FOR
LIGHT THAT'S AMBIENT
ENOUGH TO BE HELPFUL BUT
ALSO AN ARTFUL ADDITION
TO THE ROOM.

LIGHTBULB

DIMMERS ARE AN EASY
ADD-ON FOR ANY LAMP WITH
A PLUG; THEY CAN BE
BOUGHT FOR AS LITTLE AS
$15 AND THEY DRAMATICALLY
TRANSFORM ANY SETTING,
ESPECIALLY THE LIVING
ROOM, WHICH IS IN SERVICE
BOTH DAY AND NIGHT.

gotta wear shades

When lamp shopping, people tend to focus their energy solely on the base of a lamp, leaving the lampshade an afterthought (if a thought at all). But that is to overlook a light's brightest potential.

Don't settle for the inexpensive shade that often comes with the base. Fabric, silk, and high-quality paper shades are an easy upgrade. When picking a shade, bring the lamp with you to ensure a perfect match. A shade should roughly mimic the shape of the lamp's body. So a cylindrical lamp base would do well with a drum-shape shade and a curvy urn-shape base deserves a shade that flares slightly at the base.

A shade's color and opacity are factors, too. An opaque shade will direct light above and below the shade, while a sheer model will cast light through its body. Shades can be lined with pink or yellow paper to emit a soft hue (which lightbulbs can do, too).

Another way to upgrade a lamp is with its harp. A harp is the metal frame that attaches to the fixture neck and to the shade itself. It defines how high or low a shade rests on the lamp. Swapping out an ill-suited harp will help you improve the character of the lamp.

MEASURE FOR MEASURE

SHADES SHOULD BE ABOUT
THREE-QUARTERS THE
HEIGHT OF THE BASE AND
SEVERAL INCHES WIDER
THAN THE BROADEST PART
OF THE LAMP, AS YOU
SHOULD NEVER SEE A LAMP'S
BULB OR STEM.

WHY NOT TRY

ADDING A TOUCH OF WHIMSY
TO A CLASSIC LAMP WITH A
DECORATIVE FINIAL, AN
ORNAMENT THAT SCREWS ON
TO THE TOP OF A LAMP'S
HARP (OR FRAME). SPECIALTY
LAMP STORES CARRY STYLES
IN HUNDREDS OF SHAPES AND
MATERIALS.

accessories

You can arrange the furniture till you're blue in the face, but the living room won't be done until you add your own flair—which means accessories. By definition, accessories are nonessentials—throw pillows and blankets, framed pictures, books, and objects—but really, they're what makes a room look inhabited. Soft goods, like pillows and blankets, add warmth, while pictures and books add a personal note. And because they're a room's most affordable element, you can change them with the seasons. When summer rolls around, trade a woolly crimson throw for one in woven flax-colored cotton. A vibrant new set of pillows and throws can instantly revive a ho-hum living room.

The homes of avid readers tend to have piles of books in every room, but the biggest, prettiest, and most interesting titles should be saved for the living room, where a thick stack of volumes brings a sculptural touch to the coffee table. It's easy to go overboard, but when it comes to picking personal affectations, such as framed photos, act like an archivist. **Don't put everything out, just pick your favorites.** A single photograph can say more than a dozen.

USING TRAYS TO MAKE A
DISCONNECTED GROUP OF
OBJECTS SEEM LIKE A
COLLECTION.

typecasting: accessories

Rooms that are filled with accessories look alive, so don't stop at throw pillows alone.

Throw pillows. Pillows are a handy way to ratchet up a sofa's comfort level. But they're even more valuable for imbuing pattern, color, and texture. They add a big dose of style in a small package. Is there such a thing as too many? Yes! Use a sparing mix of squares and bolsters, you shouldn't have to remove pillows to get comfortable.

Throw blankets. Fold one over the edge of a modern sofa to soften severe edges or pile two or three on a bench or stool to add a burst of color.

Books. Small stacks in varying heights add architecture to your coffee table. Pick titles that reflect your interests and hobbies. And don't be afraid to undress your books by removing their glossy covers to reveal their bright fabric bindings.

RULES OF THE ACCESSORY GAME

FOLLOW THESE SIMPLE RULES AND YOU WILL SOON SEE THAT ADDING A FEW LITTLE THINGS TO A ROOM CAN MAKE A BIG DIFFERENCE.

LOVING STUFF IS NOT THE SAME AS DISPLAYING STUFF. YOU WOULD NEVER WEAR ALL OF YOUR EARRINGS, NECKLACES, AND BRACELETS AT ONCE NOR SHOULD YOU DISPLAY ALL OF YOUR OBJECTS AT ONCE.

GROUP LIKE OBJECTS TOGETHER BY COLOR, SHAPE, OR MATERIAL.

USE TRAYS TO MAKE A DISCONNECTED GROUP OF OBJECTS SEEM LIKE A COLLECTION.

USE MULTIPLES OF THINGS, BUT ALWAYS DISPLAY IN ODD NUMBERS.

PAY ATTENTION TO SHAPE. IF ALL OF THE FURNITURE IN YOUR ROOM IS BOXY THEN OPT FOR SEVERAL OBJECTS WITH SHAPELY CURVES.

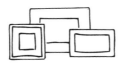

Vases and objects. Display items that mean something to you, such as decorative bowls that you picked up while traveling, an heirloom box that was handed down to you, or a Popsicle-stick sculpture made by your child. Add interesting shapes and for impact, cluster similar objects, such as vases.

Framed photos. Edit, edit, edit. Pick your favorites, frame them simply and in a similar style (such as in silver) and display a small grouping instead of scattering them throughout a room.

Flowers and plants. You don't need a green thumb to display cut flowers. Forget fancy botany; just pick whatever is freshest at the grocery store. Choose one variety of flower and get three times more than you think you need. Cut them short and arrange them in a dense bunch (see page 153).

collection notice

Collecting is a national pastime; after all, we're a culture that prizes consumption. Who doesn't love the pursuit of an object, particularly one that satisfies a personal interest, curiosity, or hobby? Collections vary enormously from sentimental to precious, from priceless to worthless. But even a dime-store collection has enormous impact when displayed as one (remember the adage, "one person's junk is another person's treasure"). **To make your doodads dazzle, follow these rules:**

1. Too much of one thing is just too much. Collections need to be edited. Act like a curator and display only your best pieces.
2. Relegate your display to one area, wall, or room; your objects have a stronger impact viewed together versus spread all over the house.
3. Think creatively when displaying collections: Shadowboxes can corral small objects while open shelves provide a surface to display larger items graphically against a wall. For hanging objects, dangle them from pretty hooks or knobs.
4. Collections of objects can have unifying features beyond their type. Group objects that have similar color, size, history, or sentimentality.

WHY NOT TRY

COLLECTING SOMETHING
AS SIMPLE AS CALLIGRAPHED
PLACE CARDS FROM ALL
OF THE DINNERS, PARTIES, AND
WEDDINGS THAT YOU'VE
ATTENDED (HEY SOMEONE
SPENT A LOT OF TIME
WRITING THOSE!).

GROUPED TOGETHER (SEE
OPPOSITE PAGE) THEY HAVE
ENORMOUS GRAPHIC IMPACT
AND APPEAL.

finishing touches

Complete the living room by **styling your side tables** with an expert touch. You don't need the eye of a stylist to make it look artful, just follow these steps.

1. BEGIN WITH A LAMP TO ADD BOTH FUNCTION AND A SENSE OF HEIGHT TO THE TABLE. MAKE SURE IT DOESN'T OVERPOWER THE SURFACE—THE LAMP BASE SHOULD COVER NO MORE THAN ONE QUARTER OF THE TABLETOP.

FOR A PERSONAL TOUCH, GROUP FRAMED PICTURES OF [FA]MILY, FRIENDS, OR PETS. DISPLAY AN ODD NUMBER—AND [N]O MORE THAN NINE. PICK A UNIFYING FRAME STYLE (SUCH [A]S SILVER, BLACK, OR WHITE), BUT ALLOW THEM TO VARY [IN] SIZE AND SHAPE.

3. TO ADD DIVERSITY AND STYLE, ARRANGE A FEW OBJECTS OF DIFFERENT SIZES, COLORS, SHAPES, AND MATERIAL. ANYTHING FROM A SMALL SCULPTURE TO A DECORATIVE BOWL TO A CLAY POT MADE BY YOUR CHILD WILL WORK.

4. BRING IT TO LIFE BY INCLUDING A VASE OF FLOWERS OR A PETITE POTTED PLANT IN AN ATTRACTIVE (NOT PLASTIC!) PLANTER. ANYTHING LIVING WILL DO—EVEN A MINI TERRARIUM OR A SINGLE GOLDFISH!

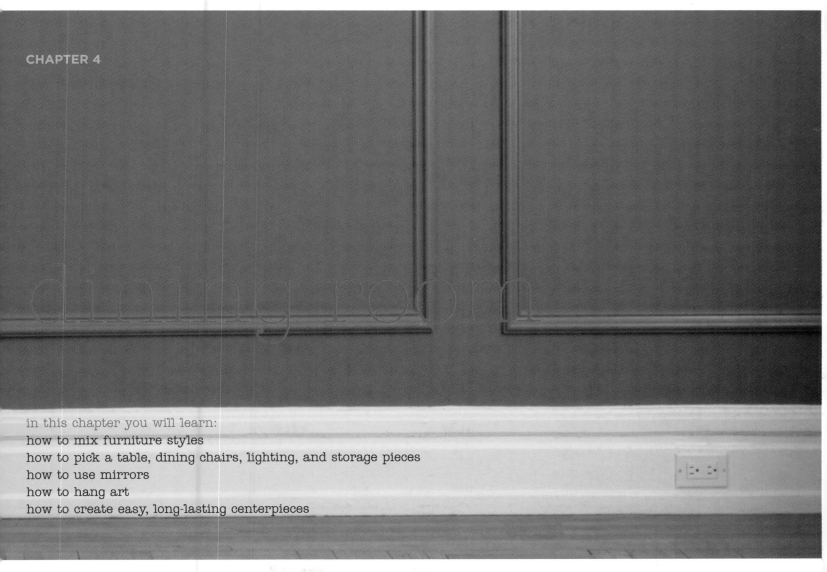

dining room

in this chapter you will learn:
how to mix furniture styles
how to pick a table, dining chairs, lighting, and storage pieces
how to use mirrors
how to hang art
how to create easy, long-lasting centerpieces

I KNEW OUR DINING ROOM WOULD HOST MUCH MORE THAN THE OCCASIONAL DINNER PARTY AND HOLIDAY MEAL. IT IS ONE OF THE MOST TRAFFICKED ROOMS IN OUR HOME.

I love to cook, but even more than that, I love to entertain, which is why when my husband and I finally bought and renovated our apartment, I insisted on having a formal dining room.

That may not seem like a big deal to those of you who live in houses with more rooms than you can count, but city dwellers like me obsess over the use of every precious square foot.

From the minute I crossed its threshold, I knew our dining room would host much more than the occasional dinner party and holiday meal. It is one of the most trafficked rooms in our home. It's where my kids spread out their art projects, where my husband and I sort mail and pay bills, and where a Monopoly marathon can extend into the wee hours.

The dining room is also the unexpected place where I perch and pace during important phone conversations. I didn't plan for it. It just so happened that the wall under the dining room window

became the last-resort home for an antique Swedish settee that had been shuffling around the house. The bench now not only hides an ugly radiator, but also provides a warm, sun-drenched spot for me to chat on the phone. And it taught me an important lesson: Decorating isn't permanent. Go with the flow. Some of the most brilliant decorating moments happen by accident.

As for the room's decor, I chose to paint it chocolate brown because: a) It's my favorite color; b) It's warm and cozy; c) It looks good with everything; and d) It's the color of a most popular dessert. The trim and ceiling are white, of course (see page 15)—it's the vanilla icing on the chocolate cake.

For the furniture, I followed one of my decorating mantras: mix and match; pair old with new, round with square, light with dark. A room of eclectic furniture is far more interesting than one that's matchy-matchy. I started by picking a table (which, along with chairs, is the only true dining-room necessity). I never considered a wood table partly because I think wood furniture can feel stodgy and partly because the floors are wood and the room is already brown. I wanted a gleaming surface that looked as crisp and clean as a pressed white tablecloth. A Parsons-style white-laminate rectangular table fit the bill; every piece of china, glass, flower, and linen looks good on it, it's easy to clean, doesn't show water rings, and doesn't need polishing. But to keep the table from looking too new and too slick I paired it with a set of old chairs. A friend of mine, decorator Miles Redd, found the six red leather upholstered French seats, which are comfortable and stainproof. Their curved backs and crackly leather make them the perfect foil for the angular and pristine table.

It might seem like a glaring oversight (pun intended) that I don't have a chandelier, but **any piece of good lighting sets the mood**, even sculptural sconces with dimmers, which are augmented with light from candles and a well-placed mirror that doubles the effect. (Unlike a chandelier, which should always hang over the centerpiece, sconces don't limit the placement of the dining table.)

The last puzzle piece was art and accessories. In the dining room, guests have only each other to admire until you add art. It doesn't so much matter what style or period of art you love, it's **how you hang art that makes it count**.

Create a big statement with a dozen little pictures, or find a wall-filling single image to captivate your audience.

dining tables

The best dinner parties have 10 guests or fewer, and so should your dining table. Ten people at a table can mean three conversations or just one. (And if your guest list is heftier, just open up the living room and turn the party into a freewheeling buffet.)

When it comes to proportion, the size of the room should dictate the size of your dining table. A good rule of thumb is that the footprint of the dining table (fully extended) should cover no more than a third of the floor's total space. Remember, you'll need room for chairs and storage—and people, too.

When shopping around, check the stability of tables by grabbing and pulling the tabletop to make sure the table doesn't wobble or sway. Then push down on one corner to ensure it doesn't flip over. (But don't attempt either maneuver if the surface is styled with crystal!)

IF THERE'S ONE THING YOU DO

WHEN YOU'RE PICKING A
TABLE, MAKE SURE THERE'S
SPACE TO SIT. SOUND SILLY?
MANY TABLES HAVE
AWKWARDLY PLACED
SUPPORTS THAT THREATEN
TO BASH INTO YOUR
GUESTS' LEGS. AND MIND
THE APRON, THAT BAND
UNDER THE SURFACE THAT
JUTS TOWARD YOUR LAP;
IT'S POISED TO CRUSH YOUR
THIGHS IF YOUR CHAIRS
ARE TOO HIGH.

typecasting: dining tables

Square and rectangular tables are well suited for the shape of most rooms (which is to say boxy), allowing the most table for the space, though circular models are more conducive to conversation because there are no blind spots like there are on a table with corners. Find a table that fits your family plus a few friends and then leave the rest to aesthetics.

Rectangle. The tried-and-true pick because its profile is a natural fit for most rooms. Look for versions with "leaves," or inserts that expand the table to twice its size or more. Make sure the leaves are easy to add and remove and that they're a precise match with the table's color and finish.

Round. The most conducive to conversation, and even allows extra people to squeeze in. The shape also breaks up the monotony of square furnishings. Some include leaves that expand to an oblong shape.

Drop leaf. Ideal for small spaces, this style folds into a slim sideboard when its leaves are collapsed. Unfortunately, the close positioning of the legs makes some diners prone to bumped knees.

Pedestal. With a single column of support, this style is far and away the most spacious for legs. The tabletop can be square or rectangular, round, or even expandable with leaves.

PANIC BUTTON

JUST FIND AN INEXPENSIVE
PARTICLEBOARD TABLE
AND THROW ON AN
OVERSIZED LINEN TABLECLOTH
THAT FALLS TO THE FLOOR.
IT'S A SPACE-SAVING
SOLUTION, TOO—USE THE
UNDERSIDE FOR STORAGE
WHEN THE TABLE ISN'T
SURROUNDED WITH GUESTS.

LIGHTBULB

NO DINING ROOM?
NO PROBLEM. THESE TIPS
MAKE HOSTING À LA LIVING
ROOM A SNAP.

• USE YOUR COFFEE TABLE AS
  THE PRIMARY SURFACE.

• PROVIDE AMPLE SEATING
  FOR GUESTS, INCLUDING
  FLOOR CUSHIONS, TOO.

• SERVE COURSES THAT
  REQUIRE JUST ONE PLATE
  AND ONE FORK.

• OFFER OVERSIZED NAPKINS.

• CLEAR SURFACES FOR
  DRINKS AND AVOID STEMS
  BY SERVING BEVERAGES
  EURO-STYLE, IN TUMBLERS.

material matters

When picking a material, think of personal taste as well as practicality. A gloss-finish wood is elegant but prone to nicks and scratches and requires a tablecloth and heat-protecting pad to shield it from scalding dinner plates. Any style table can handle wear and tear as long as you protect it with a table pad or blanket before you whip out the glitter and glue.

Wood has a warm, traditional feel. Look for quality craftsmanship, including mortise-and-tenon joints, in which one piece of wood fits into a slot in the other, or dovetail, where the pieces meet jigsaw-style. Avoid wood composites like MDF (medium density fiberboard) and particleboard, which are often poorly constructed and ultimately disposable. For varnished wood, be wary of imperfections or bubbles.

Glass-topped should be tempered making it resistant to breaking, and aim for a tabletop thickness of 3/4" or more.

Marble is a challenge to keep pristine as it scratches easily and stains unless sealed regularly; but some owners think imperfections only add to its allure. Look for solid tabletops that are finely honed and sealed.

Lacquer is a catchall phrase to describe a wood product finished in a hard, colored coating that is frequently high-gloss (true Japanese lacquer, or Japanning, is costly and rare). Laminate is a plastic or polyurethane veneer fused to a wood or MDF. Both offer a staggering choice of colors and can sometimes be customized to match a paint or fabric swatch.

WHY NOT TRY

TREATING YOUR HEIRLOOM TO
A FRESH COAT OF PAINT.
THE DINING ROOM IS OFTEN A
WASTELAND FOR HAND-ME-
DOWN BUFFETS, TABLES, AND
CHAIRS, BUT ANY DREARY
ANTIQUE CAN LOOKSMART
WHEN SLICKED WITH WHITE
(OR BLACK) PAINT. TRUST
ME, YOUR GRANDMOTHER
WOULD *WANT* YOU TO USE IT.

dining chairs

The post-meal slouch should be as enjoyable as the meal, so don't invite bony backs and prickly straw seats to your dinner table. Instead, peruse chairs that invite after-dinner lounging and avoid one-click purchasing, which is based on aesthetics alone.

Dining chairs should be easy to move for all your guests, children included. Chairs with cumbersome profiles, over-stuffed seats, or dramatically splayed legs make it tricky for guests to get in and out.

One thing that probably shouldn't be on the menu: a dining room matching suite or set. Instead, mix it up with contrasting colors and materials. Dark wood chairs? Try a marble tabletop. Antique mahogany table? Add white-frame modern chairs. A surefire way to make your dining room chic is to blend styles and finishes: old with new, light with dark, slick with aged.

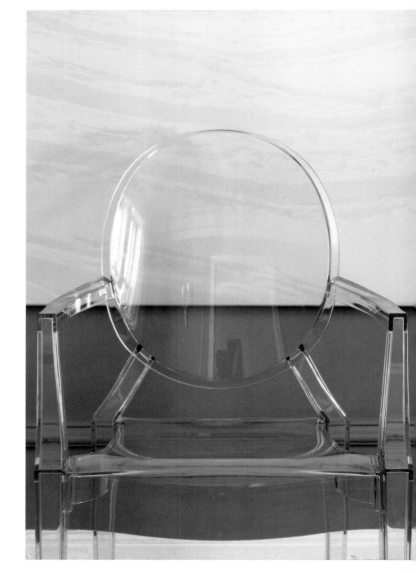

LIGHTBULB

SEATS WITH DELICATE
FRAMES, SEE-THROUGH
BACKS—OR NO BACKS
AT ALL—WON'T CLUTTER A
SMALL SPACE.

MEASURE FOR MEASURE

TO ENSURE YOUR CHAIRS
WILL FIT UNDER YOUR TABLE,
ALLOW A FOOT OF SPACE
BETWEEN THE SEAT HEIGHT
AND TABLE SURFACE. THAT
MEANS IF YOUR TABLE IS A
COMMON 29 INCHES, AIM FOR
CHAIR SEATS THAT ARE
AROUND 17 INCHES HIGH. AND
GIVE EACH DINER ABOUT 2
FEET OF ELBOW ROOM AND
AT LEAST 2 FEET OF SPACE TO
SCOOCH BACK THEIR CHAIR.

typecasting: dining chairs

Even if you don't crave a period room, consider picking from the staggering number of antique, vintage, and reproduction chairs on the market, which bring a bit of old-time grace to dinner. Or, if your table is already steeped in a legacy of its own, look to mid-century styles and beyond, which will bring an antique up-to-date. Either way, it's table first, then chairs.

Gustavian. Swedish and neoclassical with a square body, grooved limbs, and carved ornament; often painted and very feminine.

Louis–style. Named for French kings, Louis XIV has high backs and scroll arms, XV is lighter and Rococo feeling, XVI is scaled back, with tapered legs and small ornaments.

Chinese Chippendale. Thanks to its graphic fretwork back, this Asian-inspired chair (created by the famed Brit designer) looks particularly dashing in a coat of bright paint such as white, red, or even lime or turquoise.

Bentwood. Typified by the work of German-Austrian designer Thonet, these seats are simple and elegant with a curved, open back made from wood in a choice of finishes.

Tulip. Designer Eero Saarinen pioneered this comfortable molded-plastic seat that's predominantly seen in white with a brightly colored fabric seat cushion (see page 233).

Bertoia. This wire-mesh chair, named for designer Harry Bertoia, comes in a diamond or L-shape profiles and has a seat (and sometimes back) cushion and a chrome or powder-coated finish.

Contemporary. Current styles vary wildly, but a neutral, tightly upholstered L-shape chair is an all-purpose favorite.

Super-modern. Italian designers pioneered this style that uses molded plywood, acrylic, poly-blends, or metal to make high-style seats that are easy to stack and durable. The Ant chair and Philippe Starck's acrylic Louis Ghost chair (see page 122) are examples of modern classics.

WHY NOT TRY

THE OLD MAXIM IS TRUE:
OPPOSITES ATTRACT.
CONSIDER THESE FOOLPROOF
PAIRINGS FOR DINING CHAIRS
AND TABLE.

* MODERN MOLDED-PLYWOOD
  CHAIRS WITH AN OLD
  WOODEN FARMHOUSE TABLE

* WHITE-FRAME GUSTAVIANS
  AND A MODERN LACQUER
  PEDESTAL TABLE

* LOUIS-STYLE CHAIRS WITH A
  BOXY, SUPERMODERN TABLE

* DELICATE BENTWOOD
  CHAIRS AT A MODERN
  PEDESTAL TABLE

* MODERN WIRE BERTOIA
  CHAIRS WITH A ROUND
  MARBLE-TOP TABLE

material matters

The question of a chair's materials is really a question of tolerance: Are you willing to polish and scrub your chairs, or is a once-in-a-while wipe-down as far you'll go? Think about your needs first and then make sure that you're getting the best construction for your dollar.

Wood, when well made and well maintained, will last lifetimes. Pick a frame that's supported with corner blocks, which make it sturdy. Like with dining tables, look for well-crafted joints and avoid MDF and veneers, which can chip over time. Look closely for imperfections in the wood or finish.

Upholstered leather seats are long lasting and easy to clean while patterned fabrics hide stains. Many designers now turn to the newest outdoor fabrics, which are soft, stylish, and spill- and stainproof. The rules for buying a sofa (see page 64) still apply. Ask what's inside, look for hand-tied springs, and try before you buy.

Acrylic and plastic are man-made materials that require the least maintenance and are often the most durable. Many styles in this category are also stackable.

LIGHTBULB

IF YOU PURCHASE A
SLIPCOVERED CHAIR,
BUY AN EXTRA COVER OR
TWO AND STASH THEM
FOR EMERGENCIES.

typecasting: alternative seating

Don't limit yourself to a half-dozen identical chairs. Alternate the seats half and half or find six or eight (or ten!) different styles. Keep the look uniform by picking a common color or material, such as mahogany or white paint. Or forget traditional chairs altogether and try one of these.

Benches. For a casual approach that's right for speedy morning or midday meals, try dining picnic table–style. It's family-friendly and perfect for when you need to squeeze in a crowd.

Settee. This small upholstered seat typically fits just two people, making it a fun option for couples and kids. Its back support makes it a good pick for evening affairs. Try one at each end of the table.

Folding. Many of these models collapse into a thin column and store with ease. A pair can easily fit under a bed. Folding chairs often run small so look for ones with generous seats.

WHY NOT TRY

PUTTING A FAVORITE
COMFORTABLE SEAT OR
SMALL SOFA NEAR THE
WINDOW IN THE DINING
ROOM SO THAT YOU CAN
ENJOY THE ROOM
WHEN IT'S BETWEEN MEALS.

MEASURE FOR MEASURE

IF YOU'RE DARING ENOUGH
TO USE A RUG IN THE DINING
ROOM, THE PERFECT SIZE IS
ONE THAT'S FOUR FEET
LARGER THAN THE WIDTH
AND LENGTH OF THE TABLE.
THE RUG SHOULD BE
LARGE ENOUGH SO THAT THE
CHAIRS CAN MOVE AWAY
FROM THE TABLE WITHOUT
THEM FALLING OFF OF
THE EDGE. STORAGE
FURNITURE LIKE THE CHINA
CABINET OR SERVING
PIECES SHOULD BE ON THE
FLOOR, NOT ON THE RUG.

lighting

When lighting is ideal, it tends to go unnoticed, but when it's harsh—think high-school gymnasium—it'll be the only thing on your mind. Sure, lighting exists primarily to help you see, but it's also an element through which you can reveal your personality. The table and chairs establish a look. Think of those as the shirt and pants of your dining room outfit and the lighting as the jewelry. Light fixtures dress up (or down) your style.

Fixtures run the gamut from ritzy rock crystal to austere aluminum. No matter the look, when the sun sets, take a cue from your favorite restaurant and keep the lights low. If you have several light sources, keep each at a flicker. There should be enough illumination to help you get around the room, but at the table, low wattage will keep you and your guests looking attractive all the way from appetizer to dessert.

IF THERE'S ONE THING YOU DO

INSTALL DIMMERS. THEY
WORK IN EVERY ROOM, BUT
THEY'RE ESSENTIAL HERE
WHERE DIFFERENT PURPOSES
(SETTING THE TABLE VS.
DINNER ITSELF) REQUIRE
VARYING WATTAGE.
LAMPS CAN BE OUTFITTED
WITH CLIP-ON DIMMERS FOR
AROUND $15 EACH AND YOU
CAN INSTALL WALL DIMMERS
FOR SCONCES AND
OVERHEADS YOURSELF. BUT
IF YOU'RE WARY OF CROSSING
YOUR WIRES, HIRE A PRO.

typecasting: lighting

Any fixture with a lightbulb will fit the functionality bill, but dining room lighting is really a question of mood. Pick a pair of sconces or a dazzling overhead and then light candles to ratchet up the glamour.

Sconces. These wall-mounted fixtures provide pockets of light without overpowering a room. They look best when hung in pairs on the longest windowless wall in the room. Most sockets won't accept bulbs over 40 watts, but a subdued 15 watts usually does the trick, and keep in mind that a mirrored sconce will double the lightbulb's effect.

Chandelier. Choose a glitzy crystal-encrusted one or a slick, modern version. Both promise the ultimate in mood lighting, especially when fitted with clear bulbs, which help light refract.

Candlelight. Simple and elegant. For the most flattering light, let a dozen or more white votives and tea lights add brightness to a room with low-lit sconces or a chandelier.

MEASURE FOR MEASURE

TO MAKE THE MOST OF YOUR LIGHTING, HANG IT CORRECTLY. THE BULBS IN SCONCES SHOULD BE AROUND 5.5 TO 6 FEET HIGH FROM THE FLOOR AND THE BOTTOM OF A CHANDELIER SHOULD HANG ABOUT 30 INCHES ABOVE THE TABLETOP.

WHY NOT TRY

INSTALLING PINK LIGHTBULBS IN DINING ROOM FIXTURES TO BRING OUT THE ROSY GLOW OF YOU AND YOUR TABLEMATES.

wax on

There are scores of candle styles and each one sends a different message with its flicker.

Tea lights, votives, and other small, low candles are ideal for the dining table because they don't hinder eye contact.

Tapers lend a formal feel when placed in shapely silver candlesticks and are downright regal in candelabras.

Pillars, which range in height and thickness, are romantic and look especially modern when aligned in a shallow tray (see page 153).

HOW TO REMOVE CANDLEWAX FROM A TABLECLOTH

BEGIN BY CHIPPING AWAY EXCESS WAX WITH A BUTTER KNIFE, SPOON, OR YOUR FINGERNAIL.

LAY THE TABLECLOTH ON AN IRONING BOARD AND PLACE A PLAIN BROWN BAG— WITHOUT ANY WRITING ON IT— OVER THE REMAINING WAX.

APPLY A WARM IRON TO THE PAPER. THE WAX WILL ADHERE TO THE PAPER. REPLACE THE WAX-COVERED BAG AS NEEDED.

CONTINUE LIFTING WAX FROM THE CLOTH UNTIL IT IS GONE.

FOR COLORED CANDLE WAX STAINS, FOLLOW DIRECTIONS ABOVE, BUT TREAT THE SPOT WITH A PREWASH STAIN REMOVER BEFORE WASHING.

storage

Making room for storage in or near the dining room is essential because soup tureens and once-a-year silver candelabras are best kept out of precious kitchen real estate, which should be dedicated to utility.

Most dining rooms have too much space to not have storage units. Because action is centered at the table, you can dedicate at least one wall to storage without it being obtrusive. **Look for units that are roomy but not gargantuan.** Then fill it with essentials for serving and entertaining, from fine china and serving pieces to napkins, candles, and matches, so you won't have to rummage through your kitchen cabinets while dinner's getting cold.

typecasting: storage

First determine what you're storing and then decide what type of piece (or pieces) fit your needs and note the number of shelves, plus their height and depth. And make sure your choice won't overwhelm the room.

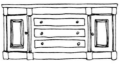

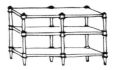

Sideboard. Long and low, this piece, often called a buffet, has covered shelves and an expansive surface for arranging flowers, candles, or objects—or serving a full-on feast. In a living room, a similar style is referred to as a credenza.

Armoire or china cabinet. This covered or glass-enclosed piece emphasizes vertical space and frames porcelain or objects while protecting them from dust. Place flatware or silver in drawers lined with felt or silver cloth; both can be bought by the yard and cut to fit.

Bookcase or étagère. An alternative to traditional storage is shallow shelving or a bookcase. Inexpensive versions are around 12 to 16 inches deep. Boxes on the shelves can house small objects while stacks of plates, nice serving pieces, and books can remain exposed.

WHAT BELONGS IN DINING ROOM
STORAGE

LINENS
(TABLECLOTHS, DINNER NAPKINS,
COCKTAIL NAPKINS)

FINE CHINA

SERVING PIECES
(PLATTERS, TRAYS, CONDIMENT DISHES)

FLATWARE AND SILVER

PLACE CARDS

CANDLES AND MATCHES

GLASSWARE AND STEMWARE
(HIGHBALL GLASSES, TUMBLERS, MARTINI
GLASSES, SNIFTERS, FLUTES, AND
WINEGLASSES)

BARWARE
CORKSCREW AND BOTTLE OPENER
ICE BUCKET AND TONGS
PAPER COCKTAIL NAPKINS)

mirrors

To bring even more drama to a beautifully lit room, hang a well-placed mirror. It will provide a stylish optical illusion, transforming even the teensiest of spaces into a glamorous parlor.

A long mirror mounted vertically draws the eye upward, accentuating height, even in a room with low or average ceilings. Hung horizontally at eye level, it'll catch light from candles or sconces and double the perception of the room. If it's hung near your guests, make sure it's flattering. It shouldn't cut you off at the neck (too high) or reflect only your midsection (too low).

Frame style should be the yin to your furniture yang. If you have a square table, pick a round mirror. If your furnishings are sleek and modern, try an ornate carved frame. If a massive sideboard sits along one wall, try mounting a series of small mirrors above it to help break up its heft. The key is for it to be proportionate with the furniture in the room— a mirror (or composition of mirrors and art) will look most pleasing if it's the same width as the furniture below it.

WHY NOT TRY

USE YOUR MIRROR TO MAKE MAGIC:

* HANG IT DIRECTLY ACROSS THE ROOM FROM A WINDOW TO DOUBLE YOUR VIEW.

* USE IT TO CHANNEL LIGHT FROM ONE ROOM INTO A DARK SPOT.

* LET IT REFLECT BEAUTY BY DIRECTING IT TOWARD FLOWERS OR ART.

* HANG A GENEROUS MIRROR AT EYE-LEVEL TO MAKE THE ROOM APPEAR BIGGER.

* ALLOW IT TO DOUBLE THE AMBIENCE IN A CANDLELIT ROOM.

IF THERE IS ONE THING YOU DO

MAKE SURE YOUR MIRROR REFLECTS BEAUTY ONLY. REMEMBER THE PHRASE, "IF YOU DON'T HAVE ANYTHING NICE TO SAY..." MY CREDO FOR MIRRORS IS SIMILAR: IF YOU DON'T HAVE ANYTHING NICE TO SHOW... THE MERITS OF A LOOKING GLASS ARE LOST IF THE ONLY THING IT REFLECTS IS A PILE OF JUNK.

hanging art

Diners are a captive audience, so hang your favorite art surrounding the table where it can provide conversation fodder and enhance a beautiful meal. Art ties a room together and adds interest and drama to empty spaces.

More often than not people hang art too high, too spaced out, or they just don't hang it at all. When mounted properly, it draws your eye up, down, and around the room. Display art that you love, be it one or two dramatic photographs or canvases, a series of postcard-size watercolors, or an antique object.

There are two ways to test picture placement:

1. Trace the frames onto Kraft paper, cut out dummies. Then tape them to the wall.
2. Use painter's tape to outline shapes and possible compositions on the wall. Live with the wall mock-up for a few days.

typecasting: hanging art

Let your room tell you what it requires from the art department. If your furniture is arranged symmetrically, mix it up with an offbeat composition. If you've already been daring with furniture shape and color, try a uniform grid. But before you grab your hammer, you should know exactly where you're going to place that nail.

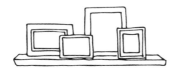

Free form. This approach works best for hanging many disparate pieces together on one wall. When pieces vary in size and shape, first arrange them on the floor and then transfer the composition to the wall. Start by placing the biggest piece, which can be at the center of off to a side. Arrange smaller works around it, keeping the same distance between frames. Make sure color and intensity is spread throughout.

Gridlock. A striking, graphic method is to hang works of identical size in an orderly grid. Determine the amount of space separating them, such as three inches, and use that as the margin around all of the frames.

Going out on a ledge. For a casual, layered feel that lets you swap out works frequently, mount one or more ledges on a wall. Lean framed art on the ledge and let the edges overlap, which gives it a carefree, bohemian vibe. A similar technique works with larger pieces arranged on a sideboard or mantel.

MEASURE FOR MEASURE

THE CENTER OF YOUR
FRAMED WORK SHOULD BE
EYE-LEVEL. OR, POSITION THE
BOTTOM OF THE FRAME
ABOUT 3 TO 6 INCHES ABOVE
A PIECE OF FURNITURE.
IF IT IS A ROOM WHERE PEOPLE
ARE SITTING, MAKE SURE
YOU TAKE THAT LOWER
VANTAGE POINT INTO ACCOUNT
AND ADJUST ACCORDINGLY.

hanging helpers

When it comes to hanging art, your eye is sometimes more helpful than a tape measure and a level. Enlist a friend to help or try it yourself with one of these easy hanging methods.

Method 1

Use a Book. When hanging a group of pictures in a cluster or grid, find a book with a binding that's the same width or height as the distance you desire between frames vertically or horizontally. Then use it as a guide to space the pictures evenly.

IF THERE'S ONE THING YOU DO

FIND A SPOT FOR PERSONAL,
FRAMED FAMILY PHOTOS (AND
THOSE OF DOGS, TOO) AND
KEEP THEM CONTAINED THERE
INSTEAD OF SPREADING THEM
THROUGHOUT YOUR HOME.

Method 2

 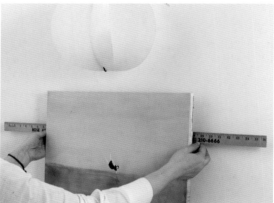

Use a Yardstick. Hammer a 1.5-inch finishing nail through the center of a yardstick, making sure that it pokes out the back end and that the head of the nail isn't completely flush with the yardstick. Hang the wire or bracket of the picture from the nail head. (Do not rest the entire weight of the picture on the nail, but enough to make sure that the wire is taut.) Point the nail at the wall, adjusting the stick until it rests where you want it to hang. Gently press the yardstick against the wall, just hard enough for the nail to make a mark on the wall. Remove the picture and yardstick and install your picture hanger; remember to adjust for the distance between the nail and the actual hook; you want the V of the hook to be exactly where your original depression is.

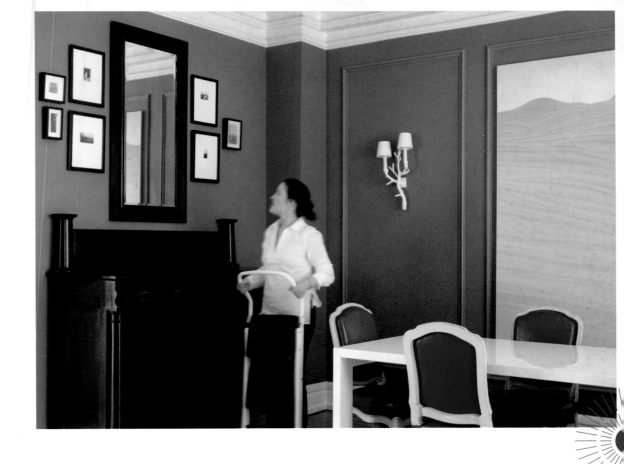

finishing touches

A bare table is an invitation to add an eye-appealing tableau. You should have a few centerpiece ideas on hand—some that expire, like fruit and flowers, and others, such as a grouping of vases, that last the whole season.

1. ONE-KIND-OF-FRUIT BOWL FEATURING JUST ORANGES, JUST APPLES, ETC.

2. AN ODD NUMBER OF SIMILAR-COLOR VASES IN DIFFEREN SHAPES AND STYLES.

A VASE FILLED WITH A SINGLE VARIETY, BUT ALWAYS AT LEAST THREE TIMES MORE FLOWERS THAN YOU THINK NECESSARY.

4. WHITE PILLAR CANDLES IN VARIOUS SHAPES AND SIZES.

5. A CONTAINER FILLED WITH GREENS FROM YOUR LOCAL MARKET OR PICK THEM FROM THE NEAREST TREE IN YOUR YARD.

family room

in this chapter you will learn:
how to make a room feel comfortable
how to choose and mix fabrics
how to store and organize media equipment
how to style a bookcase

EVEN
BEFORE
I KNEW
HOW MUCH
WE
WOULD USE
THIS ROOM,
I UNDERSTOOD
THE
KIND
OF
ATMOSPHERE
I WANTED:
LAID BACK.

Every home needs a room with no expectations, a place where it's okay to lounge, spread out, even throw your feet up on the table. In my home it's the family room, and it's the most comfortable room in the apartment.

Even before I knew how much we would use this room, I understood the kind of atmosphere I wanted: laid back. It's helpful to **know the purpose of your room and furnish it accordingly.**

The two key considerations of the family room—comfort and fabric—go hand in hand. You'll never be fully relaxed if you're terrified of staining what you're sitting on. To determine the right fabric choices, think about look, feel, and most important, durability.

In our family room there's a good mix of both patterns and scale. Many people struggle with the thought of using several prints together, but there is a foolproof way to make it work: you must **mix patterns of different scale and shape, but stay within a similar color palette.**

I know I recommended in the Living Room chapter that you upholster your sofa in a solid (see page 63), but in the case of our family room, I broke my own rule. Instead I upholstered my sofa in a brazen, colorful stripe. It's okay **to break rules, but do it for a good reason.** The print, while bold, works on this sofa for several reasons. First, it's young, fun, and lively—just like my kids. Second, its pattern hides stains. Third, the stripe running horizontally creates the illusion that the room is longer than it is. If you can come up with three good reasons to break a decorating rule, go for it.

One aspect of the family room that cannot be overlooked is the significant amount of *stuff* most families cram in here. An organized storage system is a must.

Many elements in the family room are ones that appear in the living room—think sofa, chairs, carpet. The difference here is that your purchases should emphasize comfort and durability. It should be both functional and fun, somewhere your family is clamoring to enjoy.

carpets

A feeling of comfort starts from the ground up, so make your first purchase for the family room a cozy essential: a carpet or rug. A layer of luxury underfoot is essential in a room where every element exists to help you relax. Carpet is also a must for a home with children because it provides not just a warm seat on which to spread out board games but also a soft landing pad.

While many people use the terms rug and carpet interchangeably, there is a difference between the two. A carpet tends to be wall-to-wall, or at least covering most of the room, if not stapled to the floor. A rug is freefloating and capable of rolling up. (For more info on rugs, see page 68.)

Carpets have an advantage over many rugs because most boast a generous pile, the gauge of how tall the fibers are. A shag carpet has an exaggerated high pile while Astroturf (note—not a carpet) has almost no pile. The thicker the pile, the more inviting the carpet is to sit on.

Installing a wall-to-wall requires professional assistance and a bit of a commitment—if you've soiled the carpet, only another rug (or a replacement carpet) can hide it. If your family room already has wall-to-wall carpet, don't hesitate to add an area rug on top. Even a 5 x 7-foot can slip under the front sofa legs and envelop a pair of chairs, creating an inviting sitting area in a larger room.

The choice of a solid color, textured solid, or pattern is mostly an aesthetic decision. As with all carpets, keep in mind that white and pale-colored floor coverings expose dirt while specs of lint show up on dark ones. Both textured solids and patterns bring a bit of character to the floor and hide wear and tear (like stains) with ease.

LIGHTBULB

OUTDOOR CARPETS, MADE
WITH POLYPROPYLENE AND
OTHER WATER-RESISTANT
FIBERS MAKE THEM IDEAL FOR
HIGHLY TRAFFICKED INTERIOR
SPACES, LIKE KITCHENS,
BATHS, AND HALLWAYS, AND
ESPECIALLY FAMILY ROOMS.
SOME COMPANIES (SUCH AS
DASH & ALBERT) MAKE
CARPETS THAT ARE
MACHINE WASHABLE AND
BLEACHABLE.

EDUCATED CONSUMER

TO TEST THE DURABILITY OF
A PILE CARPET THAT'S
MACHINE-MADE, FOLD IT IN
HALF, GOOD SIDE OUTSIDE.
SEE IF THE BACKING SHOWS
THROUGH. IF YOU CAN SEE
THE GLUE OR BACKING
EASILY, IT'S NOT ESPECIALLY
DURABLE.

typecasting: carpets

When shopping, think mostly about comfort but consider longevity, too.

Tufted carpets. This most common style of carpet, and also the least expensive, is at its best when made from 80 percent wool and 20 percent nylon, a reliable blend of softness and durability. In this process, loops of fiber are sewn through a backing; the more tightly packed the loops, the more longevity you can expect. The most popular finishes are: Cut pile, also known as velvet or plush pile, this finish is sheared to create short, thick, and plush carpet that's soft to the touch and has a tendency to show footprints; Loop pile, loops are kept intact, but it risks being snagged; and Cut loop and pile, contains a mix of the first two styles by which a carpet exhibits patterns with the varying texture.

Woven carpet. A minority in the carpet market, this is manufactured on a loom where back and front are linked together. Axminster and Wilton are two noted types of woven carpet.

seating

If you're lucky enough to have both a living room and family room, then your sofa choice for both will be considerably less taxing. The glory of the family-room sofa is that it can be a little bigger, a little loungier and squishier, and a little messier-looking than the more formal one in your living room (see page 60). (And you shouldn't be compelled to primp its cushions during commercials, either.) The same theory goes for chairs. A worn leather armchair brings character to the room because it looks lived-in and loved and signals that the room is meant to be used—and even beat-up a bit. The furniture in this room should never be labeled as precious. Of course, there's a fine line between well-loved and just plain the worse for the wear. Just use caution to stay on this side of the line.

EDUCATED CONSUMER

IF COMFORT IS AT THE TOP OF
YOUR LIST, HERE ARE A FEW
THINGS TO LOOK FOR:

• EXTRA-DEEP SEATS

• DOWN OR DOWN-COVERED-
  FOAM CUSHIONS

• AMPLE CUSHIONS AND
  THROW PILLOWS

• ULTRASOFT CHENILLE,
  CASHMERE, CORDUROY, OR
  WOOL UPHOLSTERY

• SLIPCOVERS, ATTACHED
  WITH ZIPPERS OR VELCRO

REALITY CHECK

IF YOU'RE TERRIFIED OF
SPILLS AND STAINS (OR ARE
SMITTEN WITH IVORY LINEN),
BUY A SOFA AND/OR CHAIRS
WITH A SLIPCOVER.
THESE ZIPABLE SHEATHS
CAN BE REMOVED AND
CLEANED AND YOU CAN
HAVE ANOTHER MADE
WITHOUT EVEN SENDING
THE FURNITURE TO THE
UPHOLSTERER'S WORKROOM.
MAKE SURE THE COVER
IS A PERFECT FIT. LIKE
SPIES, THE BEST SLIPCOVERS
GO UNDETECTED.

fabrics

By far the MVP of the family-room comfort playoffs is fabric. On top of just looking good, textiles afford the hidden pleasure of being soft to the touch—a key element in a room dedicated to relaxation.

The idea of ease comes in many fabric forms: placid colors like blue and green, soft textures such as chenille and cashmere, or homespun patterns like checks and gingham.

There are two ways that fabric choices here differ from those in other rooms. One, anything that enters the family room needs to be exceptionally durable and two, this is a spot where patterns can run free. Not only are they decorative and cozy, but also they're brilliant at masking stains.

If prints make you gun-shy, you can get similar interest from juxtaposing dissimilar fabrics, such as smooth and nubbly or soft and coarse. Velvet cushions with a leather sofa, linen with mohair, or raw silk with boiled wool are all apt combinations.

typecasting: fabrics

When throwing around fabric terms, make sure to note the difference between a weave (aka, a style of fabric) and a fiber (which is the blend of plant matter and man-made material). Velvet, for instance, is a fabric style, but can be made with fibers of silk, cotton, rayon, viscose, or a blend. In general, natural fibers such as cotton and wool have increased durability when blended with a synthetic. Only some fabrics are appropriate for covering a sofa or chair, and they're dubbed upholstery weight.
Here's a selection:

Velvet. A fabric defined by its short, dense cut pile gives this a soft, luxuriant texture and look. The cotton version is sturdy and inexpensive while the silk variety has unforgettable feel.

Chenille. A fuzzy, traditionally cotton material that has additional pile wrapped around each fiber, resulting in a remarkably soft hand.

Corduroy. Very short piles extend from the ribs (or "cords") of this fabric to make it feel almost like velvet.

Flannel. It can be as sturdy and luxurious as billiard cloth or in weaves as thin as pajamas; it's most often seen in wool, but available in cotton.

Cotton. Ubiquitous in the home market for its strength and breathability, common weaves include duck, a tough-wearing canvas and twill, which is defined by the diagonal lines on its face and its soft hand.

Linen. One of the most rugged natural fibers. Linen is cool and absorbent but wrinkles easily, which is why it's often seen in blends with cotton or synthetics.

EDUCATED CONSUMER

BEWARE OF SO-CALLED STAINPROOF FABRICS AND CARPETS. UNLESS IT'S MADE WITH SOLUTION-DYED FIBERS, RUGS AND FURNITURE ARE SIMPLY TREATED WITH A TOPCOAT OF STAIN-REPELLENT CHEMICALS. THAT MAY SAVE YOU A FEW ACCIDENTS, BUT PRODUCTS SUCH AS SCOTCHGARD ONLY LAST FOR AROUND SIX MONTHS. AFTER THAT, THE TREATMENT IS RENDERED SOMEWHAT INEFFECTIVE. FORGET THE EXTRA TIME AND MONEY FOR TREATING TEXTILES UP FRONT, INSTEAD, JUST HAVE CLEANING SOLUTION THAT'S APPROPRIATE TO YOUR FABRIC AT THE READY AND FILL YOUR HOME WITH MATERIALS SUCH AS WOOL, WHICH IS NATURALLY SPILL-REPELLENT.

Wool. The most durable of all. This fiber takes on many forms, it can be soft or scratchy, thin or thick, and can generate heat or maintain cool and it naturally resists moisture and stains.

Mohair. This supersoft fabric is woven from the hair of the Angora goat and often used in blends with wool or cashmere.

Cashmere. The lustrous wool from the cashmere goat promises over-the-top comfort but is precious—and costly.

Leather. An ultradurable, easy to maintain material that has different qualities depending on the finish. Top-quality calfskin leather ages very well.

Outdoor fabrics. Typically acrylic, the fibers in these fabrics are dyed with a solution that protects them from water, stains, and wear.

SO HAPPY TOGETHER

THE TEXTILE YOU PICK TO UPHOLSTER OR SLIPCOVER YOUR FURNITURE SHOULD HELP IT PERFORM ITS DUTIES WITH DIGNITY AND STYLE.

FOR A FOOTSTOOL THAT GETS WEAR AND TEAR: LEATHER OR OUTDOOR FABRICS

FOR A COZY READING CHAIR: MOHAIR, VELVET, OR CHENILLE

ALL-PURPOSE SOFA FABRIC: COTTON DUCK OR WOOL

FOR A SLOUCHY SOFA: CHENILLE, VELVET, MOHAIR, WOOL, COTTON DUCK, OR CORDUROY

FOR SLIPCOVERS: COTTON DUCK OR LINEN

pattern playbook

The easygoing, playful vibe of the family room makes it a perfect canvas for fabrics with pattern. Not only do prints layer visual interest into the room, but they also add a heaping dose of personality. Another reason they're prime for the family room: They're superstars at hiding dirt and stains. Layering a few patterns will bring a room interest and texture. But there are a few rules to follow if you want to avoid pattern mayhem.

First, all your fabrics should share a commonality. The easiest one is color. While textures and prints can vary, colors should stay within a defined palette. Leave room for one unexpected color to be thrown in for interest. Varying the scales (or sizes) of your patterns keeps the room harmonious. Three or four patterns should be the maximum for any room—and this includes your carpet. For foolproof pattern mixing, follow these steps.

1. **Think big.** Choose your boldest, most decorative pattern first. A large-scale floral, awning stripe, damask, or toile would all classify in this category. This pattern most likely graces your sofa or curtains or can make a smaller statement. Call this your primary print.

2. **Ground yourself.** Layer on a solid or semisolid fabric. Choose one of the colors from the primary print and find a solid fabric in any texture, such as corduroy, velvet, or linen, in that hue. This will act as a helpful grounding fabric. A pinstripe or any fabric that has a prominent ground (the solid background) and a small, quiet detail (like tiny dots) can work, too.

3. **Play the scales.** Pick one or two more complementary patterns in different scales. Again, using your primary pattern as a guide, find a stripe in a similar palette. Stripes are some of the easiest prints to layer in to a print scheme because they are unfussy and "easy to read." Just make sure that the stripe isn't so large that it fights with your primary pattern.

PRINTS CHARMING

JUST LIKE SOME COLORS CAN
BRING A MOOD TO MIND, MANY PATTERNS
CONNOTE A FEELING.

DAMASKS ARE FORMAL AND GRAND.

**CHECKS AND GINGHAM ARE EASYGOING,
CASUAL.**

FLORALS ARE ROMANTIC.

STRIPES ARE SMART AND VERSATILE.

**HAND-BLOCKED AND ETHNIC PRINTS ARE
BOHEMIAN AND ECLECTIC.**

ottomans and footstools

Durability, if not invincibility, should be a guide for choosing the small furnishings in the family room. Instead of a standard coffee table, opt for an upholstered ottoman, which can balance a tray of remotes alongside resting feet. It can be used as an extra perch, or can be rolled away (some ottomans are on casters) to make room for a board game or round of charades. Upholster an ottoman or footstool in a durable fabric such as leather, cotton velvet, or wool flannel. If you opt for a traditional table, add a footstool or two to the mix. They're perfect small seats to pull up to the coffee table and they invite ultimate comfort and manage to keep feet off the sofa. Both ottomans and footstools have varieties with built-in storage; just lift the top cushion to reveal a secret compartment.

lighting

Lighting the family room should be built around what you plan to do in the room. Installing several light sources will give your family the most flexibility. (For more on lighting, see page 94.)

If there's a movie playing nightly, install at least one strong light within reach of the sofa; that way you can flick the switch without missing any action. (And if your family room is more like a cinema, consider blackout shades for your windows, too.)

A member of the house who enjoys reading while others watch TV will appreciate a chair placed near a standing or table lamp. A metal standing lamp that swivels or has an adjustable arm, is a good choice because it directs light only where it's needed, without distracting movie-watchers.

Wall-mounted lamps or high-voltage sconces (see p. 132) can also work in here because they remove the threat of breakage that looms over tabletop ones.

CHOOSING THE RIGHT BULB

SOMETHING AS SIMPLE AS A LIGHTBULB CAN TRANSFORM A FIXTURE FROM BLAH TO BRILLIANT.

FOR READING: A THREE-WAY BULB THAT GOES FROM DAYLIGHT TO DUSK IN TWO CLICKS

TO WARM A ROOM: A TRADITIONAL INCANDESCENT BULB, THAT EMITS SOFT, YELLOWISH LIGHT

TO INTENSIFY A MODERN INTERIOR: A HALOGEN BULB THAT GIVES OFF PURE WHITE LIGHT

FOR SUBDUED AFTER-HOURS: A PINK INCANDESCENT BULB THAT GIVES OFF A SUPERFLATTERING EVENING GLOW

storage

What's even better than embracing your clutter is finding a home for it. The family room has limitless games, hobbies, and activities waiting for you—if you can find them. So if this room isn't decked out with built-ins or cabinets, then wall-mounted shelves or bookcases will answer your quest to declutter. See if you can install one shelving system against a whole wall. Two or three same-style bookcases side by side might do the trick, too. The key is to utilize as much vertical (and then horizontal) space as possible. It may seem like a lot of space to dedicate to storage, but you're creating a sense of order that'll put everyone at ease.

While some objects are okay to keep exposed—photo albums, board games, books, and maybe even DVDs—others require a catchall. Find open-top baskets or paper- or linen-covered boxes that fit neatly in your shelves. Store your miscellany here: cables and gadgets, cassette tapes, and spare remotes. Consider it contained chaos: once it's in a bin, you don't need to worry about how it looks on the inside. Use just one to two styles of storage bins to keep the look clean, because uniformity breeds organization. Once it's neatly packaged, start labeling so that you know how to find what you need when you need it.

EDUCATED CONSUMER

BEFORE YOU BUY A MESS
OF STORAGE BOXES AND
BINS, MEASURE THE DEPTH
OF YOUR SHELVES TO
ENSURE THAT THEY WON'T
OVERHANG. THE LAST THING
YOU WANT IS FOR STORAGE
TOOLS TO BECOME CLUTTER
THEMSELVES.

WHY NOT TRY

BUYING FURNITURE THAT
OFFERS AN EXTRA PLACE TO
STORE DOODADS, SUCH AS
TRUNKS, PIANO SEATS, AND
STOOLS WITH LIDS.

media storage

We've all had a precarious stack of electronics in our lives—a cable box mounted on top of the DVD player, resting on a big-box TV. It's a tower waiting to topple and one easily avoided with the advent of so many media-specific furnishings on the market.

If you love music or film and the hoards of accompanying DVDs and CDs is hindering your ability to enjoy your media or family room, spend a bit of your home cinema budget on storage. The ideal solution includes a library-style shelving for DVDs and CDs and drawers for less uniform items such as remotes, power strips, and cords. Need inspiration? Turn on your favorite flick and ask family or friends to help you get organized. You're bound to uncover a few missing favorites along the way.

LIGHTBULB

LEGOS, LINCOLN LOGS, BLOCKS, AND MORE SHOULD BE STORED LOW IN BOXES WHERE KIDS CAN REACH THEM EASILY—AND LEARN TO PUT THEM AWAY.

typecasting: media storage

Covered. A hutch, TV cabinet, or armoire promises a compartment or an adjustable shelf for every home-media gadget out there: TVs, cable boxes, media players, and stereo equipment. As these tend to run on the large size, look for a model that emphasizes vertical space and provides drawers or cabinets for media storage.

Open shelving. A substantial unit of shelves or cubbies will provide space for electronics and the flexibility to swap units in and out and rearrange. But you've got to be ultraorganized to keep this system from looking cluttered.

TV cart. Small, movable pieces such as a TV cart are good for petite spaces. While they won't hold more than the bare-bones equipment, even a compact unit will aid organization.

Sideboard. If you have a flat screen TV on a stand, you can get away with a long, low storage unit supporting the TV. It's easy enough to retrofit a credenza or buffet into a media cabinet—just cut a hole in the back panel to allow cords to escape to an outlet.

IF THERE'S ONE THING YOU DO

GET YOUR CORDS UNDER
CONTROL. UNDOUBTEDLY
THERE WILL BE A TIME WHEN
ONE OF YOUR ELECTRONIC
DEVICES NEEDS FIXING.
RATHER THAN WRANGLING
THROUGH ALL OF THE WIRES
TO FIND THE ONE THAT NEEDS
FIXING, USE TAPE OR CORD
LABELERS TO IDENTIFY EACH
CORD AND THE DEVICE IT
BELONGS TO. FOR A TIDIER
LOOK, CONSOLIDATE WIRES
WITH CABLE MANAGER COILS,
WHICH YOU CAN PURCHASE
AT ANY COMPUTER OR
ELECTRONIC STORE.

flat screens

To say that the TV is the modern-day hearth is no exaggeration, and if your family relishes their time together in front of the screen, then don't go to extremes trying to mask the room's focal point. Instead, find it a happy home. It you have a classic big-box TV, it might be open shelving or a covered hutch, but if you've delved into flat-screen territory, you have a different set of challenges.

Flat screens have revolutionized not just the way people watch TV, thanks to their high-definition plasma and LCD screens, but also the way people incorporate TV into their homes. They crop up in unexpected rooms (kitchen, bathroom) because their skinny profile is just that easy to accommodate. But most televisions, like most art, are simply hung too high. Eye-level is still the general rule, but remember, it's eye-level from where you're *viewing,* so account for your being seated, not standing up.

typecasting: flat screens

Ideally, before you purchase a TV, you'll make a kraft-paper cutout that's the identical size. (Screen measurements refer to the diagonal across the screen, so hunt down the actual height and width dimensions.) Tack that to the wall and have a seat to make sure you're not tilting your head to view the center of the make-believe screen. If the natural spot for it is too high, such as above a mantel, look for a TV that has a tilting mount, which can angle the screen downward. The brackets or mount on which your TV attaches must be drilled into the support frame of the room (i.e., the studs).

Standard mount. The TV adheres to static wall-mounted brackets.

Tilting mount. These brackets allow the screen to angle forward, which helps when it's hung high.

Articulating mount. Two extendable arms are secured to the wall mount, and to the screen so that it moves easily side to side, up, down, and tilting.

Stand. This sleek base for the flat screen is similar to that of some computer monitors. It fits comfortably on a low table, console, or buffet. This is the only method whereby you won't be drilling into the walls.

LIGHTBULB

WHEN YOU'RE BUILDING
A NEW HOME, ELECTRICIANS
CAN RUN A FLAT SCREEN'S
WIRES THROUGH THE WALL
TO AN OUTLET, BUT IF YOU'RE
ADDING ONE TO AN EXISTING
HOME, THEN CONSIDER
PURCHASING A MOUNTABLE
PLASTIC STRIP THAT DISGUISES
CORDS AND HOLDS THEM
FLUSH (AND DISCREETLY)
AGAINST THE WALL. YOU CAN
BUY THEM AT ANY HOME
IMPROVEMENT STORE.
THEN PAINT THE STRIP THE
SAME HUE AS YOUR
WALL, AND YOUR WIRE
WOES ARE OVER.

finishing touches

Inevitably in every home, bookcases become a dumping ground for papers, photos, and, of course, books. But because open shelves reveal everything (unlike desks and closets), a bit more care taken can produce a proud display. Consider backing bookshelves in colored paper or painting the back of the shelf a contrasting color. This perks up a humdrum bookshelf and helps make the objects on the shelf pop. By following a few easy styling tricks, you can turn your bookshelves into artfully arranged tableaux.

CHAPTER 2: LINE UP. LINE BOOKS UP ON SHELVES, STACKING THEM BOTH VERTICALLY AND HORIZONTALLY IN A RHYTHMIC PATTERN. THIS WILL ADD VISUAL INTEREST TO THE SHELVES AND BREAK UP THE MONOTONY OF ROWS UPON ROWS OF BOOKS.

CHAPTER 3: CONCEAL. MAXIMIZE UNUSED SPACE WITH ATTRACTIVE BOXES. BOXES ALLOW YOU TO NEATLY STORE EVERYTHING FROM PHOTOS TO COMPUTER MANUALS AND THEIR SOLID BLOCKS OF COLOR BREAK UP THE ROWS OF BOOKS.

CHAPTER 4: EMBELLISH. ADD CERAMICS AND OTHER OBJECTS FOR VISUAL INTEREST. PHOTOGRAPHS OR SMALL WORKS OF ART LEANING AGAINST A STACK OF BOOKS PERSONALIZE A BOOKSHELF AND PREVENT IT FROM LOOKING TOO STAGED.

bedroom

in this chapter you will learn:
how to choose the right size and shape bed
how to select a mattress and pillows
how to pick bedside tables, lamps, chairs, and dressers
how to keep whites white
how to create more storage space
how to make two rooms out of one
how to make a bed

EVERY
NIGHT
I'D LIE
IN BED AND
THINK,
*SOMEDAY I'LL
DECORATE THIS
ROOM . . .*
ONE DAY I
WOKE UP AND
TURNED
SOMEDAY
INTO
THAT DAY.

In my family, I'm always the last person to get dressed, the last to the dinner table, and the last to get into the car. It's not that I'm running late; it's that I'm laying out clothes, cooking dinner, and packing the bags for everyone else. So it's not unusual that our bedroom was the last room in our house to be decorated.

I know I'm not alone in this matter. Most of us—women, men, and especially parents—place ourselves at the end of a very long list of priorities. And thus, on the decorating totem pole, our bedroom was dead last. The white, bare-bones room we had lived in for years wasn't inspiring, it was plainly functional. Every night I'd lie in bed and think, *Someday I'll decorate this room…* One day I woke up and turned someday into that day. The tipping point for me was finally finding a bed I love. But you might have another motivation. The point is, **don't put it off, just get started.** Plot your first move—that'll be the first domino that sets the others in motion.

If it were decked with large swaths of fabric, my canopy-style bed would be overpowering, but I've kept the wrought-iron frame unadorned, so instead it adds architecture to an otherwise simple, sparsely furnished space. My next find was a beautiful pink woven silk-and-linen fabric—a swatch of which I carried in my bag for months. I would pull it out at lunches with friends or while sitting in bed with my husband and ask what people thought about it. **Don't be afraid to ask for help.** After seeing his reaction to the pink sofa, I wanted to make sure my husband was okay with including another rosy number in the bedroom. (He finally acquiesced once I announced my intention for pale gray walls—and white trim, of course.) So, the fabric made it onto an upholstered headboard and shades on both windows.

The existing brown wood floors felt drab and heavy in contrast to the freshness of the room. Despite having a small home office in there, the bedroom is a getaway and I wanted all the room's elements—floor included—to add to that transporting feeling. I don't gravitate toward wall-to-wall carpets and I didn't default to a sisal area rug as I often do; instead I found my answer with paint. I have loved painted floors since I was a kid. My parents had a painted bedroom floor when I was growing up. It has the same effect as wall-to-wall, but it is easier to maintain and I don't have to worry about pet accidents. For my current bedroom I chose a checkerboard pattern to give the illusion of the room being larger.

Other furniture took less thought. The bedside tables are the same ones we've had since we were newlyweds. My motto is, if it ain't broke, don't fix (or change) it. I don't see the point in splurging on a new pair (they'll just end up covered in books anyway). The tables and swing-arm reading lights mounted above them are the same on both sides of the bed. I haven't advocated for matching sets elsewhere in the house (in fact, I've encouraged you to *avoid* matching), but there's a reason it works in the bedroom: symmetry is calming. Unlike rooms for entertaining where you and your guests get a kick out of witty mix-and-match schemes, the bedroom should be ruled by peace and order.

The final and biggest task of my bedroom redo was to create a wall of door-covered, built-in cabinets, which took the place of a dresser and armoire. This is an expensive option, but was an essential for storing linens, towels, and clothing. I also enlisted the cabinetmaker to make a unit for my computer and a pullout keyboard tray. Would I prefer a stand-alone office? Of course, but an office that disappears behind covered doors was the next best thing. If you must make a sacrifice, do so stylishly. Oh, and there was one more tidbit—I covered my Saarinen tulip chair cushion with a kicky yellow fabric. Every room should have something out of the ordinary to keep things lively.

beds

Pick a bed frame that sends a message the second you walk in the door. In this room, a dynamic bed is 80 percent of the decorating. The rest of the room can be modest or even unremarkable as long as the jewel of the setting is top-notch. For a romantic, that might mean curlicues of wrought iron while it's a sleek low-slung platform style for a modernist. At all costs, avoid a mattress pushed against the wall; there really is nothing more depressing.

Start by choosing a bed size. **Think twice before going grander than queen—you'll need a lot of space** (and a big washing machine) for that California king. To gauge the total footprint of the bed, add about a foot perimeter to the mattress dimensions (which allows for bed frame and coverings) and block it out with tape or a paper cutout on your bedroom floor. Give yourself another foot around the cutout, which is enough room for walking around and making the bed. Optimally, the final dimension won't take up more than one-third of the total floor space and won't block doors or windows. As for height, eyeball it. If you have a low ceiling, don't buy a bed that is heavy-feeling or too tall.

Ideally, your bed should face something pleasant such as a window or a placid piece of art, and be accessible on both sides. Do your best to keep busy surfaces out of sight. A clutter-induced panic attack is no way to start a morning.

typecasting: beds

When choosing a bed, keep in mind that the bigger the mattress, the trimmer the frame should be. It shouldn't look like it's swallowing the room. Headboard styles that peak in the center and slope on the sides (similar to a camelback sofa) are an optical illusion that makes the mass of the bed seem minimized by drawing the eye up at the center. And a white-painted frame is lighter-feeling than a mahogany box.

Canopy. Ideal for a room with high ceilings, this bed often has swags of material attached to a frame overhead. This cozy, romantic style was originally conceived to keep sleepers warm, but modern takes that come without a fabric dressing are streamlined and architectural.

Platform. A low-slung frame with no headboard, posts, or ornaments, which is why modernists admire it. At worst, this style can be a tad cumbersome, so for petite rooms, pick a platform with a receded kick space to give the illusion of a floating mattress.

Four-poster. This classic pick defines your sleeping space with posts that can be carved wood or pared-down metal. To keep the bed from overwhelming the space, aim for posts that are no higher than two-thirds of the room's ceiling height.

PANIC BUTTON

GET AN UPHOLSTERED
HEADBOARD, WHICH ADDS
COMFORT AND CAN BE
REUPHOLSTERED TO SUIT
CHANGING STYLES.

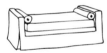

Headboard. A traditional shape that can be rendered in a number of materials, such as wood and upholstery. It should measure 48" by 60" high (higher if you have a box spring), which is enough to support you when you sit up. The headboard (or footboard) can also act as a partition.

Daybed or trundle. Daybeds and trundles are usually pushed flush against the wall. Both styles typically accommodate twin-size mattresses, but some versions have an additional twin that pulls out to double the size or storage drawers tucked under the frame. This is a great bed for kids or rooms that do double duty, like a home office or guest quarters.

MEASURE FOR MEASURE

A HANDY GUIDE FOR
MATTRESS SIZES.

• DOUBLE IS 54" X 75"

• QUEEN IS 60" X 80"

• KING IS 78" X 80"

• CALIFORNIA KING IS 72" X 84"

mattresses

You've heard the spiel before: "Your mattress is the most important purchase you'll ever make"; "You spend a third of your life on it"; but the real reason buying a mattress is tricky is that no one can do it for you—only you know what's right. The choice is highly subjective: What's comfortable for one person might not be for another.

Browse mattresses in person. Ultimately you can buy one online or over the phone, but first you have to sleep around. If you're sharing the bed, invite your partner, and bring along your pillows. Lie down for at least ten minutes in your normal sleep position. The mattress should gently support your body at all points and keep your spine in the same shape as if you were standing with good posture. Never rely on labels to tell you which mattress will give you the right support; instead, go by feel.

REALITY CHECK

NOT SURE IF YOU NEED A
NEW MATTRESS?
HERE'RE FIVE TELLTALE SIGNS.

• YOU WAKE UP WITH ACHES
AND PAINS.

• YOU SLEEP BETTER IN BEDS
OTHER THAN YOUR OWN.

• YOU CAN SEE DEPRESSIONS
IN YOUR MATTRESS WHERE
YOU USUALLY SLEEP.

• YOU CAN FEEL THE COILS.

• YOU HAVE HAD YOUR
MATTRESS FOR MORE THAN
TEN YEARS.

typecasting: mattresses

There is no best kind of mattress, only personal preference for feel and price.

Innerspring. This most common type gives support from metal coils, but it's not the number of coils, it's the gauge (aka, thickness) of the coil that determines its firmness. The heftier the gauge, the stiffer the mattress, the thinner the gauge, the springier the mattress. (Remember that the lower the gauge number, the more durable the wire. For example, 12-gauge wire is thicker than 14-gauge wire.)

Foam. This style is filled with a combination of natural and synthetic fibers. Expect to pay top-dollar for memory-foam or Visco-elastic foam styles, which mold to the contours of your body.

Pillow-top. An extra layer of foam or stuffing atop this mattress increases comfort, but not necessarily longevity (though you can still wrestle at least eight years out of it). Most experts recommend that you regularly flip your mattress, but a pillow-top makes it a one-sided affair.

Box springs. Mattresses and box springs are actually designed to work in tandem, specifically, a box spring prolongs the life of your mattress. Be wary of trying to save money by buying a mattress without a box spring. This shock absorber provides consistent support and helps reduce the motion you feel when you or your partner toss and turn. But box springs, like mattresses, wear out. If you lie directly on your box spring and it feels uneven or you roll toward the middle, then you know you need a new one.

IF THERE'S ONE THING YOU DO

KEEP YOUR MATTRESS
(AND YOUR BODY) SHIPSHAPE
BY FLIPPING AND TURNING
IT ONCE PER MONTH FOR
THE FIRST THREE MONTHS
AND EVERY THREE
MONTHS AFTER THAT.
A MATTRESS PAD OR COVER
WILL PROTECT THE
FABRIC AND FOAM LAYERS
FROM MOISTURE AND GRIME.

pillows

Just like choosing a mattress, picking a pillow is a matter of taste—it's your personal lap of luxury. While most people focus on a pillow's stuffing (i.e., down, synthetic, wool, or cotton) it's the density—soft, medium, or firm—that's critical for comfort.

To determine the right density for you, consider how you sleep. The goal for all sleepers is to keep your neck and spine straight and supported, but each sleep style has a unique need: Stomach sleepers need the least support, back sleepers need medium support, and side sleepers need the firmest support.

Stuffing is important when it comes to shelf life. A top-quality goose-down pillow is the long-distance champ, lasting around five to eight years, while synthetic pillows expire sooner, in one to three years. Here's a simple test for down pillows: Fluff the pillow, fold it in half and squeeze out all of the air, if it doesn't spring back, then it's time to replace it. For synthetic fill, check for lumpiness, i.e., spots where the filler has separated. And, as a general rule, if you're constantly wrestling with your pillow, kick it to the curb.

To make new pillows last, shop for ones with quality ticking, which is what encloses the filling. Feather or down pillows usually have tightly woven ticking so that feathers don't escape. A tight weave also helps keep out dust mites. All pillows benefit from a protective cover. The simple cotton case zips over your pillows to add an extra barrier from dirt, moisture, and dust mites. Best of all, they're washable.

WHICH PILLOW IS RIGHT FOR YOUR SLEEPING STYLE

BACK SLEEPERS
NEED: TO BOLSTER THE NECK.
PILLOW: A MEDIUM-DENSITY PILLOW OR A CYLINDER-SHAPED PILLOW UNDER THE NECK (A ROLLED-UP TOWEL ALSO WORKS). A PILLOW PLACED UNDER THE KNEES MAY ALSO RELIEVE PRESSURE ON THE LOWER BACK.

SIDE SLEEPERS
NEED: TO FILL THE GAP BETWEEN THE HEAD AND BED THEREBY EASING THE STRESS ON THE NECK AND SHOULDERS. SIDE SLEEPERS SHOULD AIM TO KEEP THE HEAD AND SPINE IN A HORIZONTAL LINE.
PILLOW: TRY A CONTOURED OR MEMORY FOAM-STYLE PLUS ONE PLACED BETWEEN THE KNEES TO STACK THE HIPS IN PROPER ALIGNMENT.

STOMACH SLEEPERS
NEED: REQUIRES THE LEAST SUPPORT—JUST COMFORT.
PILLOW: A THIN, SOFT PILLOW THAT LIGHTLY CUSHIONS THE HEAD AT A NATURAL ANGLE.

typecasting: pillows

Only one pillow per person is truly an essential, but making an indulgent bed requires more pillow power. Here are the four key styles of cushions in order of placement from headboard forward.

European square: 26" x 26". A foundation that provides support for sitting up or reading in bed.

Standard pillows: 20" x 26". This size suits your sleeping pillows as well as a pair of shams, the decorative pillowcases.

Boudoir pillow: 12" x 16". A petite decorative pillow that is generally centered in the pillow arrangement.

Neck roll: Its size varies, but this cylinder-shaped pillow is also decorative.

WHY NOT TRY

ARRANGING THE PILLOWS TO
SUIT YOUR STYLE. ON A FULL
OR QUEEN BED, TRY THE
FOLLOWING.

MODERN: ON EACH SIDE,
TWO BEDROOM PILLOWS
STACKED FLAT (NOT ANGLED)
ON TOP OF EACH OTHER.

TAILORED: TWO TILTED
OR STANDING EURO
SQUARES, THEN A PAIR OF
STANDARD SHAMS LEANING
AGAINST THOSE, AND
FINALLY A STANDARD
PILLOW EACH.

ROMANTIC: THE SAME AS
TAILORED, BUT ADD A
BOUDOIR PILLOW AND A
BOLSTER IN FRONT.

sheets

A well-made bed of fresh, tautly pulled sheets is the embodiment of ultimate comfort. It transports you, makes you feel better, and takes just five minutes each morning to make.

To simplify things, take cues from your favorite hotel and go white. While patterned and solid-color sheets tend to fade or look tired after so many washes, plain whites (and those with embroidery detail) can stay crisp and fresh for years. Plus, with no patterns or colors to coordinate, making the bed is a snap. Mix and match your whites and you'll never know the difference. Inject color and pattern on the curtains, Euro-square pillows, or with a throw blanket, but for sheets, keep it a whiteout.

PANIC BUTTON

IF YOU'RE TOO CRAZED TO MAKE HOSPITAL CORNERS BEFORE RUSHING TO WORK, DO AWAY WITH THE FLAT SHEET AND BLANKET COVER AND PULL UP THE DUVET AND DUVET COVER ONLY.

LIGHTBULB

IF YOU'RE INTO MATCHING, FOLD AND STORE SHEET SETS INSIDE ONE OF THE PILLOWCASES SO YOU CAN GRAB AND GO.

EDUCATED CONSUMER

THINK OF THREAD COUNT AS
THE S.A.T. SCORE OF
SHEETS—IT MAY INDICATE
QUALITY, BUT IT'S HARDLY A
CONCISE MEASURE OF
BRILLIANCE. THE TERM
THREAD COUNT REFERS TO
HOW MANY FIBERS ARE IN
THE COMBINED WARP
(VERTICAL) AND WEFT
(HORIZONTAL) OF ONE INCH
OF FABRIC. THREAD
COUNTS RANGE FROM 80
TO 700 AND THE COMMON
MISNOMER STATES THAT
THE MORE THREADS PER
INCH, THE SOFTER THE
FABRIC. BUT IT'S THE QUALITY
OF THE FIBERS THAT
DETERMINE FEEL, WHICH IS
WHY 180-COUNT FINE
COTTON FEELS BETTER THAN
A 400-COUNT IN MEDIOCRE
MATERIAL. (SOME
MANUFACTURERS SNEAKILY
TWIST TWO SUPERFINE
FIBERS TO DOUBLE THEIR
THREAD COUNT NUMBERS.)
BY THREAD COUNT
ALONE, A 180 TO 200 COUNT
SHEET WILL OFFER
COMFORT AND DURABILITY,
ESPECIALLY 100 PERCENT
PIMA OR EGYPTIAN COTTON
OR WORDS LIKE SUPIMA
(A TYPE OF PIMA) OR PERCALE,
ALL OF WHICH DESCRIBE
HIGH-QUALITY MATERIAL.

typecasting: sheets

A sheet wardrobe typically includes:

Fitted sheet. The foundation of the bed has elasticized corners to help it fit snugly over the mattress. Pillow-top mattresses require deeper corners so look for labels such as High Profile or Deep Pocket, which stretch to be 12" to 18" in depth.

Flat sheet. A rectangle of fabric that is sometimes adorned with decorative embroidery or a scalloped edge.

Blanket covers and matelassés. For light warmth. These covers are stiff, flat, and crisp and traditionally used to keep the bed clean.

Duvet cover. This envelops a fluffy down duvet. Keep poofy and messy covers like this folded in thirds at the foot of the bed.

Shams. The same shape as the standard pillow, but this case has an additional flange of fabric around the pillow perimeter. These turn standard pillows into decorative statements.

Pillowcases. A cover for your sleeping pillow, plain and simple.

Box spring cover. If your box spring is exposed above the bed frame, this decorative fitted sheet camouflages it.

Bed skirt. Also called a dust ruffle. This flounce of fabric hangs over the base of the bed frame to near the floor, which is ideal for hiding under-bed storage.

WHITES DONE RIGHT

HOW DO YOU KEEP WHITES WHITE? HERE'S A LAUNDRY LIST OF WAYS:

ALWAYS INSPECT BEDDING FOR STAINS BEFORE WASHING; TREATING THEM AS SOON AS POSSIBLE IS A MUST. THE LONGER A STAIN SITS, THE QUICKER IT SETS, WHICH NOT ONLY CAUSES DISCOLORATION, BUT ALSO WEAKENS THE FABRIC. ALWAYS WET THE STAINED AREA WITH COLD WATER FIRST, THEN SPRAY IT WITH A STAIN REMOVER. CHECK THE SHEET LABELS FIRST AND THEN USE THE HOTTEST TEMPERATURE THE FABRIC CAN WITHSTAND. THE HOTTER THE WATER, THE MORE EFFECTIVE THE DETERGENT.

DON'T WASH WHITES WITH COLORS. THE NUMBER ONE CAUSE OF DINGINESS IS BLEEDING FROM COLORED MATERIAL. THE SECOND CULPRIT IS DETERGENT RESIDUE, WHICH IS A MAGNET FOR DIRT. YOU NEED LESS DETERGENT THAN YOU THINK, SO READ THE DIRECTIONS ON THE BACK OF THE BOTTLE. AND FOLLOW YOUR MACHINE'S INSTRUCTIONS TO ENSURE PROPER WATER LEVELS AND RINSING.

CHECK BEDDING FOR STAINS BEFORE DRYING. DRYING A STAINED AREA WILL BAKE THE STAIN INTO THE FABRIC. IF A STAIN DOES NOT GO AWAY AFTER ONE WASHING, THEN TREAT IT AND WASH IT AGAIN AND AGAIN UNTIL IT'S GONE.

AVOID CHLORINE BLEACH. BLEACH BREAKS DOWN OPTICAL BRIGHTENERS (CHEMICALS THAT ARE APPLIED TO WHITE TEXTILES THAT KEEP THEM LOOKING WHITE) AND WEAKENS THE FIBERS. OVER TIME BLEACH WILL LEAVE WHITES LOOKING GRAY OR YELLOW. LOOK FOR DETERGENTS THAT HAVE ADDED OPTICAL BRIGHTENERS; THEY WILL REPLACE WHAT IS STRIPPED OFF IN WASHING.

lighting

Pinpoint where you need illumination and then seek the ambient or task lighting necessary. Chances are you won't be riffling through your wardrobe at the same time that you are tucking in for the night with a book, so choosing a few points of light is the best approach. Overheads tend to cast shadows, so avoid these in favor of a few strategically placed lamps, especially bedside. Night owls with partners should get a lamp with an opaque shade, which directs light exactly where you need it and allows you to read even if your partner is catching ZZZs. And remember that the most important aspect of any bedside light is that you can turn it off without getting out of bed.

typecasting: lighting

Bedroom fixtures should create pools of light exactly where you need them: bedside, dresser, closet, and desk. Overhead lights tend to cast shadows, so avoid these in favor of a few well-placed lamps.

Table lamp. Living room–size drum and urn lamps need not apply; this lamp should be diminutive because its sole task is to brighten your bedtime activities.

Task lamp. A clip-on or wall-mounted version is the simplest way to free up valuable bedside table real estate. Many wall fixtures have an extendable arm that lets you position the light exactly where you need it. Install these versions around 9 to 10 inches from the bedpost and around 18 inches from the top of the mattress.

Floor lamp. An alternative to the traditional picks, a floor lamp, especially one with a gooseneck, can hover over the bedside or desk.

SO HAPPY TOGETHER

SOME NIGHTSTANDS AND LAMPS LOOK
MORE INTERESTING WHEN PLACED
TOGETHER:

A METAL GARDEN TABLE WITH AN
APOTHECARY LAMP

A MODERN CUBE WITH A GOURD-SHAPED
TABLE LAMP

A DARK WOOD NIGHTSTAND WITH
CLEAR-GLASS-BASE LAMP

A SKIRTED TABLE WITH CLASSIC
SWING-ARM LAMP

bedside tables

As the bedroom has evolved from sleeping chamber to library, entertainment center, and more, the number of accoutrements burdening the once-spare bedside table has increased. Avoid a clutter catastrophe by choosing a nightstand ample enough for your needs and then invite only the necessities, such as a lamp, alarm clock, and glass of water to the prime bedside real estate. Relegate remotes, sleep aids (masks and earplugs), and jewelry or contact lenses to a drawer or container. **Your bedside table is a reflection of your habits.** If you're an avid novel reader, consider using a small bookshelf for overflow books. If you tend to pay bills in bed, find a linen box to store your checkbook and pens.

In most rooms it's imperative to mix up your furnishings and keep it eclectic, but the bedroom is one place where a matching pair of bedside tables (and even lamps) is a good idea. **Symmetry is orderly, and order is calming.**

Of course, don't go overboard and purchase a matching bedroom suite. If you already own one, split the set into different rooms, paint one piece to differentiate it, or even change the hardware to make it unique.

MEASURE FOR MEASURE

BEDSIDE TABLES SHOULD
BE LEVEL WITH THE
MATTRESS HEIGHT OR NO
MORE THAN 6 INCHES ABOVE
IT. PLACE THE TABLES A
FEW INCHES AWAY FROM
THE BED—CLOSE ENOUGH TO
BE CONVENIENT BUT NOT
TOO CRAMMED IN THAT
IT'LL IMPEDE YOUR CHANGING
THE SHEETS.

typecasting: bedside tables

Choose your nightstand for both aesthetics and function. If you have a very boxy platform bed, why not try a curvaceous pedestal table? Take inventory of your evening necessities and then find a night table with plenty of room for them.

One-drawer. This standard nightstand has a single storage compartment and sometimes a low shelf that's helpful for books or storage. A traditional shape that can be rendered in a number of materials, such as wood and upholstery.

Pedestal table. Its delicate profile is a nice counterpoint to the heft of a bed but you'll need to be a neatnik in order to keep this petite surface from getting overwhelmed.

Skirted table. Hide a multitude of sins (like stacks of folders, books, or boxes) under the fabric of this table. On top, a piece of glass fitted to the table size or a tray can make it look polished.

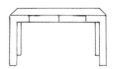

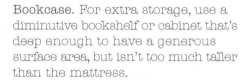

Bookcase. For extra storage, use a diminutive bookshelf or cabinet that's deep enough to have a generous surface area, but isn't too much taller than the mattress.

Chair or stack of books. A modern alternative to a traditional table. A chair or stool at the right height can add interest to the bedside. A pile of large coffee-table books, spines out, creates an artful column.

Desk. Position a simple Parsons table so that a portion of it can hold bedtime necessities while the bulk of it is dedicated to a home-office station.

storage

More often than not, your bedroom is also your dressing room. But without suitable storage, your wardrobe is liable to take over the room like kudzu. To keep clothing craziness at bay, dedicate one wall of the bedroom to storage furniture like dressers and armoires. **The important thing is that the furniture fit your needs.** If you're dress-obsessed, then make room for hanging racks and ditch the bureau. If you live in wool-sweater territory, prepare to store bulky knits. To be ultraorganized, insert dividers into drawers to wrangle small items, and add canvas shelves in your closet to give shoes and accessories a dedicated home.

typecasting: storage

Don't skimp on putting storage solutions in the bedroom, especially if it's home to your wardrobe. Just like in the kitchen, the more space there is for your possessions, the more streamlined your routine will be.

Dresser. This essential often has smaller drawers on top for items like undergarments and jewelry, and larger compartments for clothes. Plastic inserts will help divide drawers to your liking. A pair of tall, skinny dressers can also do the job of one bulky piece.

Armoire. This freestanding wardrobe is a chic way to store hanging and folded clothing, though it calls for a room with a grand scale. Make sure the hanging portion is at least 24 inches deep; many antique examples are too shallow to house conventional hangers.

Freestanding rack. For the closetless, this is a miracle worker. Creating a stylish tent wardrobe is as simple as fitting a wire rack or hanging rod with a fabric shell (especially one similar to your wall color); it's a discreet solution.

SNEAKY STORAGE

THINK YOU'VE MAXED OUT YOUR SPACE? THINK AGAIN! THE BEDROOM PRESENTS A FEW ADDED PLACES TO SQUEEZE STORAGE WITHOUT THE BULK OF MORE FURNITURE. TWO OBVIOUS PLACES: UNDER THE BED AND AROUND DOORS AND WINDOWS.

DON'T UNDERESTIMATE WHAT YOU CAN FIT UNDER YOUR BED. USE LONG, SHALLOW PLASTIC TUBS WITH SNAP-TIGHT LIDS TO STORE SEASONAL GOODS LIKE SWEATERS AND OUTERWEAR AS WELL AS CLOTHING AND ACCESSORIES WORN ONLY OCCASIONALLY (LIKE SKI BOOTS OR BLACK-TIE GARB). CONTAINERS WITH CASTERS MAKE RE- TRIEVING ITEMS A BREEZE. SUITCASES AND BOXES OF OUTDATED FILES ARE ALSO GOOD CANDIDATES FOR UNDER THE BED. TO DOUBLE YOUR STORAGE WITHOUT ADDING ANY VISUAL HEFT, PLACE RISERS UNDER THE FRAME'S LEGS (AND ADD A SIMPLE BED SKIRT).

SHELVING NEAR WINDOWS AND DOORS. SHELVING THAT FRAMES A WINDOW OR DOOR BECOMES PART OF THE ARCHITECTURE OF THE ROOM. TRY MOUNTING SHELVES VERTICALLY ALONGSIDE A WINDOW OR SKIMMING THE TOP OF A DOOR FRAME. IN EITHER CASE, THE BUSINESS OF BOOKS, BOXES, OR OBJECTS IS OVERLOOKED IN FAVOR OF A LARGER FOCAL POINT, SUCH AS A VIEW OF THE OUTDOORS OR A PASSAGE TO THE NEXT ROOM.

FOOT OF THE BED. IN LIEU OF A BENCH HERE, TRY A CHEST FOR EXCESS CLOTHING, COMFORTERS, AND BLANKETS. YOU CAN EVEN CLEVERLY OUTFIT THE CHEST TO ACCOMMODATE HANGING FILE FOLDERS AND PAPERWORK.

Closet. Make every square inch count by inserting shelving or simply hanging canvas shelves— such as for shoes or knits—from the rod. A closet that's at least 7½ feet tall can house two rods (one on top of the other); just make sure that the lowest one is around 42 inches above the floor.

CLOSET ORGANIZING 101

FOLLOW THESE SIX STEPS.

EDIT. DONATE OR TOSS CLOTHES YOU DON'T WEAR.

MAXIMIZE SPACE. INSTALL SHELVES, RACKS, BOXES, AND HANGING BAGS TO UTILIZE EVERY SQUARE INCH OF YOUR CLOSET.

HANG IT UP. INVEST IN GOOD QUALITY HANGERS; THEY WILL PROLONG THE LIFE OF YOUR CLOTHING BY HELPING TO MAINTAIN ITS SHAPE.

KEEP LIKE ITEMS TOGETHER. GROUP LIKE TYPED CLOTHING TOGETHER, I.E. ALL BLOUSES, ALL SWEATERS, AND THEN GROUP THEM TOGETHER BY COLOR, I.E. ALL BLACK, RED, ETC.

STORE SMART. KEEP ITEMS YOU USE FREQUENTLY AT EYE LEVEL OR BELOW AND THOSE ITEMS YOU RARELY USE HIGH OR OUT OF REACH.

BOX IT. USE LABELED BOXES OR BINS TO KEEP LIKE ITEMS TOGETHER AND MAKE SURE YOU RETURN ITEMS TO THEIR PROPER PLACE AFTER USE.

flooring

The bedroom floor should do one of two things: add to the crisp, clear, and uncluttered look of the room, or bring warmth and quiet. An area rug muffles noise and provides texture underfoot and is, in most cases, easier to clean and maintain than wall-to-wall. If you have wood floors, you might opt for a cozy 3' x 5' rug at the bedside to keep your feet from touching a chilly floor in the morning. White-washed wood floors are a savvy alternative to ivory carpets (especially for families and pet owners) and still bring the illusion of stepping on a cloud. (For more on carpets and rugs, see pages 68–75.)

WHY NOT TRY

PAINTING YOUR BEDROOM FLOOR. IT'S A STYLISH CURE-ALL FOR AGING FLOORBOARDS, BRINGING A GLOSSY LUSTER FROM WALL TO WALL. IT'S ALSO A BIG UNDERTAKING, SO KEEP THESE THINGS IN MIND:

• PREPARE TO SLEEP ELSEWHERE UNTIL THE FLOOR HARDENS, AROUND FIVE NIGHTS. LIKE A MANICURE, WHAT SEEMS DRY IS USUALLY STILL TACKY AND PRONE TO SMUDGING.

• MEASURE THE ROOM TO KNOW HOW MUCH PAINT TO BUY.

• PURCHASE PAINT THAT'S SPECIFICALLY FOR FLOORS, AND GET ENOUGH FOR TWO COATS.

• HAVE THE FLOORS SANDED BEFORE APPLYING A BASE COAT.

• USE A POLYURETHANE TOPCOAT TO SEAL IT AND ADD A PROFESSIONAL FINISH.

chairs

Make room for one all-purpose chair in the bedroom. In addition to being a peaceful spot for reading, resting, or putting on shoes, it can double as a desk chair. It's also a convenient place to toss clothing when getting dressed (or undressed) as well as spare pillows at night.

From a decorative perspective, a chair adds color, pattern, and shape to an otherwise boxy room. An upholstered chair can tone down the severity of those lines and introduce a soft spot. A petite upholstered slipper chair is a versatile choice as is a bench at the foot of the bed (see p. 221), and, if space allows, an indulgent chaise lounge. A master bedroom with room to spare should consider adding a footstool and lamp near that chair to make a reading nook that's more private than one in the living room.

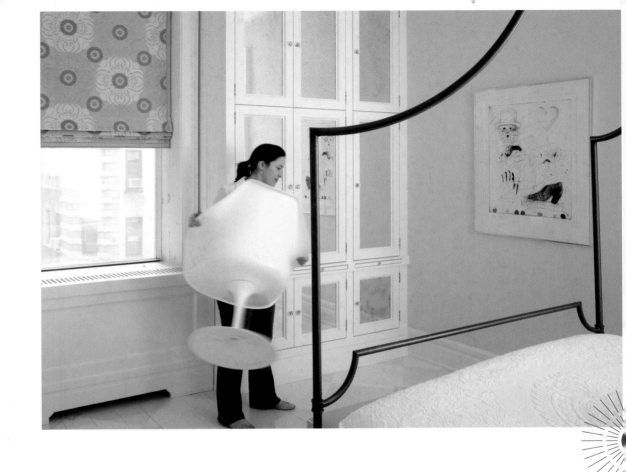

workspaces

Of the litany of jobs we demand from the bedroom—
dormitory, wardrobe, storehouse, etc.—there's one more:
home office. How did your bills end up in the bedroom?
Perhaps because it's such a placid retreat and makes the
chore of bill paying less tedious. But work and rest are
not good bedfellows. Remember this: A workspace that
won't threaten to overrun a blissful bedroom is a
workspace that disappears on command. That means
that every component—computer, papers, and supplies
included—must be able to go undercover.

SMART WAYS TO ADD OFFICE ELEMENTS TO THE BEDROOM INCLUDE:

LAPTOP COMPUTER. IT FOLDS DOWN TO A SLIVER AND USES MUCH LESS ELECTRICITY THAN A DESKTOP MODEL (UP TO 90 PERCENT).

FABRIC- OR PAPER-COVERED FILE FOLDERS AND BOXES TO ERADICATE STACKS OF PAPERS AND MAGAZINES. TO MINIMIZE THE LOOK, PICK A NEUTRAL OR A COLOR THAT BLENDS WITH YOUR WALLS.

MAKE YOUR DESK DOUBLE AS A DRESSING TABLE BY HANGING A MIRROR ABOVE THE SURFACE AND KEEPING MAKEUP AND JEWELRY IN A DECORATIVE BOX WITHIN ARM'S REACH.

MAKE A TRAVEL BIN THAT'S A MOVABLE OFFICE. USE A TOTE, CART, OR BOX THAT CAN BE MOVED TO FAMILY ROOM, KITCHEN, OR ELSEWHERE. GROUP LIKE ITEMS, SUCH AS YOUR CHECKBOOK, WITH PENS AND STAMPS. WHEN IT'S TIME TO PAY UP, JUST GRAB THAT DEDICATED BUNDLE AND GET TO WORK.

typecasting: workspaces

The core of every office is an all-purpose surface. In the bedroom, this table will ideally recede, flip up, or tuck away so that you won't be face-to-face with work when it's time to hit the pillows.

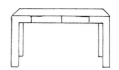

Secretary. This traditional hutch has low drawers, eye-level cabinets and a waist-level plane that unfolds into a writing surface and reveals compartments or drawers for small accessories like paper clips and stamps.

Cabinet or cube. Some designs built specifically for a home office include a slide-out keyboard tray or writing surface.

Desk. Instead of an old wood clunker, try a streamlined Parsons table with one drawer for desk knickknacks. To increase storage, add a rolling filing cabinet cube underneath. The file keeper can be painted to match the bedroom scheme or the whole desk can be fitted with a pretty skirt. Simple linen or resin boxes on top will keep bills and papers tidy.

LIGHTBULB

IF SPACE IS AN ISSUE,
CONSIDER HIRING A
CARPENTER TO CREATE A
COMPACT BUILT-IN
WORKSPACE, COMPLETE
WITH DESK AND SHELVES.
THIS IS AN EXPENSIVE
OPTION, BUT ONE YOU WILL
NEVER REGRET. JUST MAKE
SURE THAT YOUR DESIGN
INCLUDES DOORS SO THAT
YOU CAN CLOSE UP THE
SPACE AT NIGHT; YOU DON'T
WANT TO HAVE FITFUL
NIGHTS STARING AT YOUR
PILES OF PAPER!

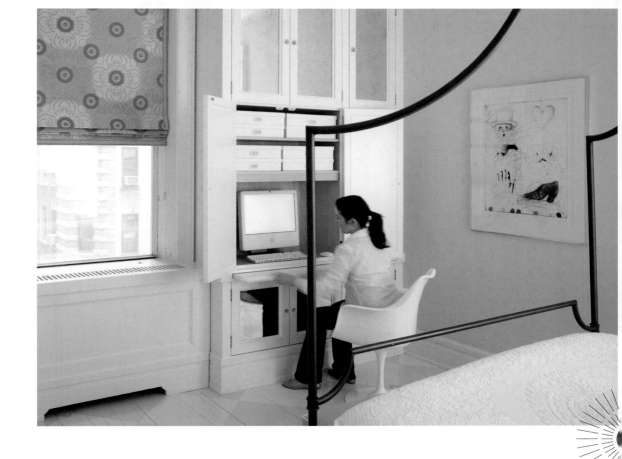

finishing touches: making a bed

Of all the silly things with which we waste time (surfing the Net, idly shopping, reality TV), saving five minutes each morning to make the bed is one act that's actually most rewarding. Start your day this way and by bedtime you'll be swooning for shuteye.

1. PLACE A FLAT SHEET, WRONG SIDE UP, ON TOP OF A FITTED SHEET.

2. LAY A BLANKET COVER OR MATELASSÉ ON TOP OF THE SHEET, ABOUT FOUR INCHES DOWN FROM THE TOP OF THE FLAT SHEET.

3. FOLD THE FLAT SHEET OVER THE EDGE OF THE BLANKET TO REVEAL ANY PATTERN OR DECORATIVE BORDER.

4A–C. TUCK THE BOTTOM EDGE OF THE SHEETS AND BLANKET UNDER THE MATTRESS AND MAKE "SQUARE CORNERS" BY GATHERING EXCESS FROM THE SIDES AND TUCKING UNDER THE MATTRESS.

5. FOLD A QUILT OR COMFORTER INTO THIRDS AND LAY AT THE FOOT OF THE BED.

6. ARRANGE SHAMS, AND STANDARD PILLOWS. ADD NECKROLL OR BOUDOIR PILLOW IF DESIRED.

1.

2 AND 3.

4A.

4C.

5.

6.

acknowledgments

My thanks, love, and respect . . .

First and foremost to my patient family who has put up with my impulsive need to repaint, reupholster, and rearrange the world around me. To my mother, Janey Schecter, who taught me everything I know and who was able, with a moment's notice, to whip up the incredible illustrations in this book. To my father, Robert Schecter, for always supporting both of us. To Tricia Davey, without whose gentle nudging I would have never made it through this process. To Vanessa Holden for initially capturing my vision so clearly. To Sophie Donelson for her solid research and for helping me transfer my words and ideas to paper. To Pamela Cannon and Random House for taking a chance on me and for allowing me to pursue my vision. To Annie Schlechter for her keen eye and uncanny ability to spot a mustache. To Dylan Chandler, for his digital prowess and fantastic organizational skills. To Mark Hartman for coming out of retirement and for being my heavy lifter. To Giorgio Baravalle for giving *Flip!* a fresh face. To Connie Newberry (and Tom) for graciously opening your doors to me when I was in need of the color red (and whenever I am in need of a big kitchen)! To Vicki Love Salnikoff for always helping me find the art I love and want to keep. To Miles Redd and Robert Lindgren for their decorating expertise. To Marian McEvoy for showing me that to love what you do is the best way to succeed in a career. To Stephen Drucker for welcoming me back in the doors of *House Beautiful*. To everyone at the *Today* show, for making me a part of your family. To Toby Young, Anita Calero, and my other fellow Virgos—only you really ever understand. To Mary Elizabeth Lawrence and Amanda Potters for your sound advice and friendship. To the ladies of D.V.—thank you for not complaining when I answered a work call or sent an e-mail from the chairlift!

about the author

Elizabeth Mayhew is the lifestyle expert for NBC's *Today* show and is special projects editor for *House Beautiful* magazine. Previously she was editorial development director at *Real Simple* magazine. A native of Louisville, Kentucky, she now lives in New York City with her husband and two children.

PHOTO: ANNE SCHLECHTER

resource guide

LOVE FINE ART INC.
535 WEST 23RD STREET S. 6N
NEW YORK, NY 10011
212-989-2029
WWW.LOVEFINEARTINC.COM

MAI 36 GALERIE
RAMISTRASSE 37
8001 ZURICH
SWITZERLAND
+41 (0) 44 261 6880
WWW.MAI36.COM

SONNABEND GALLERY
536 WEST 22ND STREET
NEW YORK, NY 10011
212-627-1018
WWW.SONNABENDGALLERY.COM

WINSTON WACHTER FINE ART
530 WEST 25TH STREET
NEW YORK, NY 10011
212-255-2718
WWW.WINSTONWACHTER.COM

YANCEY RICHARDSON GALLERY
535 WEST 22ND STREET
NEW YORK, NY 10011
646-230-9610
WWW.YANCEYRICHARDSON.COM

BED LINENS:

BED, BATH, & BEYOND
800-462-3966
WWW.BEDBATHANDBEYOND.COM

GARNET HILL
800-870-3513
WWW.GARNETHILL.COM

LANDS' END
800-963-4816
WWW.LANDSEND.COM

LEONTINE LINENS
800-876-4799
WWW.LEONTINELINENS.COM

MATOUK
WWW.MATOUK.COM

SCHWEITZER LINEN
800-554-6367
WWW.SCHWEITZERLINEN.COM

FABRIC:

CHELSEA EDITIONS
232 EAST 59TH STREET
NEW YORK, NY 10022
212-758-0005
WWW.CHELSEAEDITONS.COM

COWTAN AND TOUT
111 EIGHTH AVENUE SUITE 930
NEW YORK, NY 10011
212-647-6900
WWW.COWTAN.COM

DONGHIA
256 WASHINGTON STREET
MOUNT VERNON, NY 10553
914-662-2377
WWW.DONGHIA.COM

HINSON
2735 JACKSON AVENUE
LONG ISLAND CITY, NY 11101
718-482-1100

HOLLAND & SHERRY
979 THIRD AVENUE
14TH FLOOR
NEW YORK, NY 10022
212-355-6241
WWW.HOLLANDSHERRY.COM

RALPH LAUREN HOME
888-379-POLO
WWW.RALPHLAURENHOME.COM

ROGERS & GOFFIGON LTD.
41 CHESTNUT STREET
GREENWICH, CT 06830
203-532-8068

OUTDOOR FABRIC:

HOLLY HUNT GREAT OUTDOORS
HOLLY HUNT
979 THIRD AVENUE, SUITE 503/605
NEW YORK, NY 10022
212-755-6555
WWW.HOLLYHUNT.COM

OUTDOORFABRICS.COM
800-640-3539
WWW.OUTDOORFABRICS.COM

PERENNIALS
888-322-4773
WWW.PERENNIALSFABRICS.COM

FURNITURE:

BAKER FURNITURE
800-592-2537
WWW.BAKERFURNITURE.COM

CAPPELLINI
52 WOOSTER STREET
NEW YORK, NY 10012
212-966-0669
WWW.CAPPELLINI.COM

CHELSEA TEXTILES
979 THIRD AVENUE, SUITE 914
NEW YORK, NY 10022
212-319-5804
WWW.CHELSEATEXTILES.COM

COUNTRY SWEDISH
979 THIRD AVENUE, SUITE 1409
NEW YORK, NY 10022
212-838-1976
WWW.COUNTRYSWEDISH.COM

HICKORY CHAIR
P.O. BOX 2147
HICKORY, NC 28603
828-324-1801, EXT. 7295
WWW.HICKORYCHAIR.COM

LEE INDUSTRIES
402 WEST 25TH STREET
NEWTON, NC 28658
800-892-7150
WWW.LEEINDUSTRIES.COM

MITCHELL GOLD + BOB WILLIAMS
210 LAFAYETTE AT KENMORE SQUARE
NEW YORK, NY 10012
212-431-2575
WWW.MITCHELLGOLD.COM

NIERMANN WEEKS
232 EAST 59TH STREET
NEW YORK, NY 10022
212-319-7979
WWW.NIERMANNWEEKS.COM

OLY STUDIO
2222 FIFTH STREET
BERKELEY, CA 94710
775-336-2100
WWW.OLYSTUDIO.COM

PLEXI-CRAFT
514 WEST 24TH STREET
NEW YORK, NY10011
212-924-3244
WWW.PLEXI-CRAFT.COM

LIGHTING AND LAMPSHADES:

ARTEMIDE
46 GREENE STREET
NEW YORK, NY 10013
212-925-1588
WWW.ARTEMIDE.US

CHRISTOPHER SPITZMILLER
336 WEST 37TH STREET
NEW YORK, NY 10018
212-563-1144
WWW.CHRISTOPHERSPITZMILLER.COM

CIRCA LIGHTING
877-762-2323
WWW.CIRCALIGHTING.COM